Resisting Citizenship

Migrants squats are an essential part of the 'corridors of solidarity' that are being created throughout Europe, where grassroots social movements engaged in anti-racist, anarchist and anti-authoritarian politics coalesce with migrants in devising non-institutional responses to the violence of border regimes. This book focuses on migrants' self-organised housing strategies in Europe and the collective squatting of buildings and land.

In these spaces contentious politics and everyday social reproduction uproot racist and xenophobic regimes. The struggles emerging in these spaces disrupt host-guest relations, which often perpetuate state-imposed hierarchies and humanitarian disciplining technologies. The solidarities and collaborations between undocumented and documented activists in these radical spaces enable possibilities for inhabitance beyond, against and within citizenship. These do not only reverse forms of exclusion and repression, but produce ungovernable resources, alliances and subjectivities that prefigure more livable spaces for all. The contributions to this book address these struggles as forms of commoning, as they constitute autonomous socio-political infrastructures and networks of solidarity beyond and against the state and humanitarian provision.

The chapters in this book were originally published as a special issue of *Citizenship Studies*.

Deanna Dadusc is Senior Lecturer in Criminology at the School of Applied Social Science at the University of Brighton, UK. She conducts research on the criminalisation of migrants' solidarity and of urban struggles. Her research and teaching are informed by anti-racist and feminist approaches.

Margherita Grazioli is postdoctoral research fellow in the Urban Studies unit of the Social Sciences Department of the GSSI (Gran Sasso Science Institute, L'Aquila, Italy). She has conducted research about housing rights movements and policies in Rome, Italy, through activist ethnographic methodologies.

Miguel A. Martínez is Professor of Housing and Urban Sociology at the IBF (Institute for Housing and Urban Research) at Uppsala University, Sweden. He has conducted studies about urban sociology, housing, social movements, migration and participatory-activist methodologies. He is the author of *Squatters in the Capitalist City* (Routledge, 2020).

Resisting Citizenship

Migrant Housing Squats Against State Enclosures

Edited by
**Deanna Dadusc, Margherita Grazioli and
Miguel A. Martínez**

LONDON AND NEW YORK

First published 2021
by Routledge
2 Park Square, Milton Park, Abingdon, Oxon, OX14 4RN

and by Routledge
52 Vanderbilt Avenue, New York, NY 10017

Routledge is an imprint of the Taylor & Francis Group, an informa business

British Library Cataloguing-in-Publication Data
A catalogue record for this book is available from the British Library

ISBN13: 978-0-367-75599-7 (hbk)
ISBN13: 978-1-003-16316-9 (ebk)

Typeset in Minion Pro
by codeMantra

Publisher's Note
The publisher accepts responsibility for any inconsistencies that may have arisen during the conversion of this book from journal articles to book chapters, namely the inclusion of journal terminology.

Disclaimer
Every effort has been made to contact copyright holders for their permission to reprint material in this book. The publishers would be grateful to hear from any copyright holder who is not here acknowledged and will undertake to rectify any errors or omissions in future editions of this book.

Contents

Citation Information

The chapters in this book were originally published in the *Citizenship Studies*, volume 23, issue 6 (August 2019). When citing this material, please use the original page numbering for each article, as follows:

Chapter 6
Migrants' inhabiting through commoning and state enclosures. A postface
Massimo De Angelis
Citizenship Studies, volume 23, issue 6 (August 2019) pp. 627–636

For any permission-related enquiries please visit
http://www.tandfonline.com/page/help/permissions

Contributors

Deanna Dadusc is Senior Lecturer in Criminology at the School of Applied Social Science at the University of Brighton, UK. Her research explores the criminalisation of social movements, including the repression of squatting and of migrants' solidarity.

Massimo De Angelis is Professor of Political Economy and Social Change at the University of East London, UK. He is the author of several publications on values struggles, capitalist enclosures and the commons.

Margherita Grazioli is postdoctoral research fellow in the Urban Studies unit of the Social Sciences Department of the GSSI (Gran Sasso Science Institute, L'Aquila, Italy). Her main research interests are urban geography, housing policies and urban social movements, nurtured by her activism within Housing Rights Movements in Rome.

Miguel A. Martínez is Professor of Housing and Urban Sociology at the IBF (Institute for Housing and Urban Research) at Uppsala University, Sweden. He has conducted studies about urban sociology, social movements and participatory-activist methodologies.

Marta Stojić Mitrović is ethnologist and anthropologist working as an Assistant Research Professor at the Institute of Ethnography SASA, Belgrade, Serbia, where she researches discourses, policies and practices related to the topics of migration, citizenship, human rights and discrimination in Serbian, regional and the EU context.

Nicola Montagna is Senior Lecturer in Sociology at Middlesex University, UK, and has researched on social movements, radical activism, far right, urban conflicts, international migration, borders and migration policies.

Valeria Raimondi is PhD candidate in Urban Studies at the Gran Sasso Science Institute at the Department of Social Sciences, L'Aquila, Italy. She has a master's degree in Geography and Territorial Processes (University of Bologna, Italy).

Travis Van Isacker is PhD candidate in the School of Applied Social Science at the University of Brighton, UK, and obtained his MA in Critical and Creative Analysis from the Department of Sociology, Goldsmiths, University of London, UK.

Ana Vilenica is urban and cultural researcher and an accomplice in housing and No Border struggles. Among her research interests are cultural and political action against dominant housing regimes and other 'urban regeneration' schemes, new mutations in functioning of migration regimes as well as potentials for organising against neoliberal movement.

Introduction: citizenship as inhabitance? Migrant housing squats versus institutional accommodation

Deanna Dadusc, Margherita Grazioli and Miguel A. Martínez ⓘ

ABSTRACT
This special issue focuses on migrants' self-organised strategies in relation to housing in Europe, namely the collective squatting of vacant buildings and land. In particular, the contributions to this special issue differentiate between shelter provided in state-run or humanitarian camps and squatted homes. Migrants squats are an essential part of the 'corridors of solidarity' that are being created throughout Europe, where grassroots social movements engaged in anti-racist, anarchist and anti-authoritarian politics coalesce with migrants in devising non-institutional responses to the violence of border regimes. In these spaces contentious politics and everyday social reproduction uproot racist and xenophobic regimes. The struggles emerging in these spaces disrupt host-guest relations, which often perpetuate state-imposed hierarchies and humanitarian disciplining technologies. Moreover, the solidarities and collaborations between undocumented and documented activists challenge hitherto prevailing notions of citizenship and social movements, as well as current articulations of the common. These radical spaces enable possibilities for inhabitance beyond, against and within citizenship, which do not only reverse forms of exclusion and repression, but produce ungovernable resources, alliances and subjectivities that prefigure more livable spaces for all. Therefore, these struggles are interpreted here as forms of commoning, as they constitute autonomous socio-political infrastructures and networks of solidarity beyond and against the state and humanitarian provision

Introduction

'I am not so concerned with how we dismantle the master's house, that is, which set of theories we use to critique colonialism; but I am very concerned with how we (re)build our own house, or own houses ' (Simpson 2011, 32).

Borders are often defined as 'a tool of exclusion' which aim to 'demarcate a coherent inside from a chaotic outside' (Rajaram and Grundy-Warr 2007), and Europe is often defined as a *fortress* (Geddes 2001; Carr 2015). Yet, concepts such as *exclusion* and *fortress* allude to a clear-cut between inside and outside, that runs the danger of missing the complexity of border dynamics, and of obscuring the way borders work as tools not simply to exclude, but to control and govern the movement and lives of migrants and non-migrants alike (Mezzadra and Neilson 2013). The often arbitrary distinctions between migrants and refugees, for instance, illustrates one of the manifold devices to regulate and oppress these social groups. Borders are not only geographical demarcations of the institutional police-run checkpoints between Nation-states. If we adopt a broader sociological and political view, we find borders in everyday racist and xenophobic encounters: they are performed in the lack of access to health, housing, education, safety, work (Anderson, Sharma, and Wright 2009). Furthermore, they discipline everyday social interactions and the possibilities for acting, thinking and feeling outside of multiples forms of social control. Therefore, the extension and proliferation of borders allows to conceive them as *border regimes* (Casas-Cortes et al. 2015). Accordingly, the increasing criminalization of migration and of borders crossing functions as an ordering principle, where borders operate not as walls but as filters (Vaughan-Williams 2009) and through modes of differential inclusion (Mezzadra and Neilson 2013). Their porosity configures a technique to filter and regulate migration flows and to govern migrants' lives once the border is crossed. However, that porosity is also due to the various social struggles that rupture and create cracks in the ways borders regimes operate.

As much as borders are multiplying and extending to every aspect of migrants' lives, so are forms of resistance and everyday struggles. In the last years, across Europe, groups of migrants have been organizing themselves to resist the current migration regime and the politics of borders (Ataç, Rygiel, and Stierl 2016; Casas-Cortes et al. 2015; Stierl 2018). Anti-deportation campaigns, undocumented-workers protests, no-border camps and the constitutions of autonomous urban spaces led to the encounter and synergy between a variety of social movements contesting urban borderlands as well as the boundaries of citizenship. Beyond their claims of making citizenship-associated rights accessible to everyone regardless of their status, these grassroots movements feature forms of contentious politics that had been rarely acknowledged (Nicholls and Uitermark 2017).

This special issue focuses on migrants' self-organised strategies in relation to housing in Europe, namely the collective squatting of vacant buildings and land, either public or privately owned. In particular, the papers of this special issue differentiate between shelter provided in state-run and humanitarian camps and squatted homes. While a growing body of literature discusses migrants struggles facing an increasing criminalization and illegalization, little attention is given to the challenges they pose to what Walters (2010) defined as *humanitarian borders*. Rather than providing an alternative to securitisation policies (implemented by both military and paramilitary forces), humanitarian borders are mostly organized along racialised, colonial and economic hierarchies (Papadopoulos, Stephenson, and Tsianos 2008; Mezzadra and Neilson 2013) which contribute to the management of migrants' bodies and lives. Therefore, this special issue argues that occupations by migrants, and the various forms of solidarity with local activists, challenge the violent regime of all borders, including the so-called *humanitarian* ones, as these entail various forms of domination, discipline and repression.

The contributions to this special issue also contend that the practice of squatting by illegalised and marginalised migrants engenders actions that question normative discourses and practices of citizenship. A previous issue in *Citizenship Studies* (Maestri and Hughes 2017) placed the focus on 'camps, borders and urban encounters' as sites where the politics of citizenship are both contested and enacted. Along similar lines, when migrants squat new sites of contestation are created and new forms of political subjectivity are enacted by *making space* (Dikeç 2013; Tazzioli 2015; Ikizoglu Erensu 2016) vis-à-vis exclusionary spaces and growing restrictions to the freedom of movement and settlement. Following recent discussions on the dialectics between *the common* and *enclosures* in contested city-borderscapes (Papadopoulos, Stephenson, and Tsianos 2008; Harvey 2012; Hodkinson 2012; Mezzadra and Neilson 2013; Stavrides 2016; Mudu and Chattopadhyay 2017), this special issue focuses on the specific socio-spatial struggles of migrants' squats as practices of urban commoning and inhabitance, which situate themselves outside and against forms of control of the state and of humanitarian forms of assistance.

Housing is here interpreted as a terrain of struggle which opposes to emergency shelters and humanitarian camps. On the other hand, the creation of housing squats by people on the move can be addressed as forms of resistance to European bordering regimes and as acts of citizenship that produce antagonist political subjectivities. Indeed, squatting is primarily an *illegalised* practice for the re-appropriation of vacant spaces that results in the creation of dwelling and venues for the mobilisation of a variety of social and political struggles (Hodkinson and Chatterton 2006; Cattaneo and Martínez 2014). This way squats give life to urban networks of political contestation and experimentation in the *here and now*, where grassroots forms of self-management, solidarity and autonomy are constituted (Dadusc 2019a; Raimondi 2019; Montagna and Grazioli 2019). In these spaces everyday lives and socio-spatial relations are re-arranged in sharp contrast with the regulations imposed by racist and xenophobic regimes. Therefore, these struggles are interpreted here as forms of commoning, as they constitute livable spaces, autonomous socio-political infrastructures and networks of solidarities beyond (and against) the state and humanitarian provision.

Moreover, the relations and collaborations between undocumented and documented activists challenge hitherto prevailing static notions of citizenship and social movements, as well as current articulations of the common. Indeed, through migrants' squats different subjectivities, politics and positionalities enmesh. This heterogeneity changes the social composition of current struggles and questions otherwise unspoken hierarchies and privileges due to citizenship status. This mutual cooperation also entails a deep reformulation of local activists' relation to the state and its institutions. While this is not a smooth process, it leads to the production of forms of commoning 'within, against and beyond citizenship' (De Angelis 2019, 628), and to the constitution of 'hybrid political subjectivity between migrants and non-migrants' (Raimondi 2019, 568).

In this special issue the contributors engage with the notion of inhabitance to divert from the notion of *rights* and *citizenship*. Lefebvre (2003) poses a distinction between inhabiting (*habiter*) and habitat (*habitat*). *Habitat*, on the one hand, is conceived as a fixed container and 'springs from a strange kind of excess: a rage for measurement and calculation' (161), where urban planners give priority to functional arrangements of life: eating, sleeping, working, consuming. *Habiter*, on the other, expresses a process of making urban and social spaces (Elden 2004), namely everyday practice and social relations that escape and exceed attempts to plan, capture and govern. *Habiter*, or inhabitance, is that which will always overflow, and it is often translated as *living*. This resonates with Lefebvre's distinction between 'the city' and 'the urban', the latter characterised by encounters, density, creativity, unpredictable messiness. Drawing on Lefebvre's concept of inhabitance, we address migrants' struggles as a crucial manifestation of bottom-up production of the urban space, including housing.

According to Lefebvre, the *right to the city* is not a right to habitat, but a broader practice, that embraces forms of inhabiting. Although Lefebvre's *right to the city* framework has often been understood as merely focused on the liberal agendas of claiming equal rights, it illuminated the everyday practices of all the residents and users of space, regardless of their citizenship status (Attoh 2011; De Souza 2010; Purcell 2014; Rolnik 2014), oriented towards needs and aspirations rather than formal rights. The right to the city is the possibility to refuse to *stay put* within fixed and calculated spaces, and instead to fully exist by creating alternative socio-spatial relations and new ways of living together. The forms of inhabitance enacted through migrants' protests and through occupation of land and vacant buildings, do not only reverse the exclusion they experience, but produce ungovernable resources, alliances and subjectivities that prefigure more livable spaces for everyone.

In accordance with the above remarks, our theoretical framework contributes to ongoing debates within critical citizenship and border studies, in particular those related to the *acts of citizenship* and the *autonomy of migration*. Both approaches have provided a fertile ground and fresh conceptual tools for radical rethinking and theorising contemporary migrant struggles. The following sections will introduce these conceptual tenets in order to provide the readers with more tools for navigating the articles that we assemble here: acts of citizenship; autonomy of migration; inhabitance and home-making through mobile and housing commons; and the links between squatting and migrants' struggles. The concluding section briefly summarises the main contributions to this special issue.

Resistance to securitarian and humanitarian enclosures

As the so-called "Arab Spring" bursted in the 2010s, migration became interrelated with the financial crisis unfolding since 2008. In an uncanny parallelism, human mobility was framed as a matter of economic crisis, flows to be curbed, controlled, and rescaled. As years 2015–2016 registered a peak in the deadly shipwrecks in the Mediterranean Sea, the approaches to the global political situation that has been defined as 'refugee crisis' have been twofold, ranging between criminalization and humanitarian approaches. On the one hand, the European Union and European national governments exploited the fears generated by both the "crisis" framework and the attacks by Daesh associates, by further criminalizing migrants, framing them as a threat and implementing emergency security measures (Bosworth and Guild 2008; Aas 2011; Bowling 2013). On the other, the constitution of *humanitarian borders* (Walters 2010) has framed the condition of migrants as a humanitarian emergency, thereby legitimising their forced immobility (Ticktin 2011; Pallister-Wilkins 2017; Garelli and Tazzioli 2018). Besides, it sets up a new bordering regime while curtailing the moves of most migrants across European territories. In this context, autonomous forms of solidarity that reject the humanitarian and institutionalised management of migration are criminalised as facilitators of illegal immigration (Dadusc and Mudu 2019 – forthcoming).

Whereas borders fuel discontent, rage and potential resistance among displaced and immobilised populations, humanitarianism has the role of taming, channeling and subtly repress this discontent (ibid). Despite being framed as neutral and a-political, humanitarianism participates in the articulation of multiple relations of power that reinforce, rather than challenge the operation of borders (Ticktin 2011; Pallister-Wilkins 2018). Interventions based on charity and humanitarian assistance establish forms of dependency and perform soft modes of disciplining and control of migrants' bodies, voices and struggles. These intervene on the migrants bodies, organizing their food provision, their circulation, their mental health as well as channeling their discourses and possibilities for action (Fassin 2011; Ramadan 2013). Therefore, both securitisation and humanitarian approaches frame migration as an emergency problem to be fixed and keep refugees and illegalized migrants in a *state of exception*.

Contemporary migrant struggles resist both the politics of securitarian borders and the bio-politics of humanitarian assistance that operate within camps and emergency shelters. Migrants' occupations and self-constructed settlements emerge where there is a lack of state and humanitarian interventions (Stojić Mitrović and Vilenica 2019) as well as in direct opposition to these (Dadusc 2019b; Van Isacker 2019). These forms of self-organisation prefigure a no-border world opposing the racialised violence of borders, a world where state and humanitarian interventions are rejected and become obsolete. The networks of solidarity constituted in occupied spaces, moreover, do not reduce migrants to passive, docile or marginal subjects, but rather, place them as 'central protagonists in the drama of composing the space, time, and materiality of the social itself' (Mezzadra and Neilson 2013, 159).

Migrants' squats are an essential part of the *corridors of solidarity* that are being created throughout Europe, where grassroots social movements with anti-racist, anarchist and anti-authoritarian politics unfold non-institutional responses to the oppression of migrants: 'From sea rescue to solidarity cities, from access to housing to medical care and fair working conditions, from legal counselling to protection against deportation: we prefigure and enact our vision of a society, in which we want to live'.[1]

These corridors enable possibilities for inhabitance not only at the physical border-zones of Europe but also along the radical networks of solidarity for safe passage throughout the territory, exceeding national boundaries. The forms of solidarity emerging in these spaces disrupt the host-guest relations, which often perpetuates state-imposed hierarchies and categories (Squire and Darling 2013). Moreover, squatted spaces put the voices and needs of migrants at the forefront, and migrants and supporters tend to relate to each other as equals - a far cry from the saviour/victim relationship which exists between the givers and receivers of humanitarian aid (Dadusc 2019b).

Acts of citizenship

Extending upon Agamben's scholarship, critical migration scholars have taken up his conception of *bare life* to delineate the plight of refugees and unauthorized migrants, who exist in an indefinite and suspended state of non-citizenship (Rajaram and

Grundy-Warr 2004; Salter 2008). Accordingly, the illegalisation of migration creates a political limbo, where people's lives are held both 'inside and outside the juridical order' (Agamben 1998, 27), where migrants are denied the right to have rights (Arendt 1973) and the right to (political) existence. This view has been contested by the literature on the *acts of citizenship*, as it poses citizenship as the precondition for any form of political subjectivity. Literature and debates on *acts of citizenship* (see Isin and Nielsen 2008; McNevin 2011; Nyers 2015) place the focus on the formation of political subjectivities by those performing and prefiguring citizenship despite their exclusion from normative citizenship.

Acts of citizenship are conceptualised as collective forms of political mobilisation by undocumented/illegalised migrants who claim the *right to have rights* (Arendt 1973), and pose demands to the state and political institutions, despite their formal impossibility to claim rights. The *acts of citizenship* perspective highlights the contested politics of citizenship, arguing that practices and experiences of migration are generative of new forms of political subjectivity (Nyers 2015). Here citizenship is defined not as a formal property that can be held or given, nor as a settled identity, but as a practice that people produce through social, political and cultural modes of mobilisation (Isin and Nielsen 2008).

Isin (2008) distinguishes *acts of citizenship* from *habitus*, where enacting citizenship is intended both as having the courage of breaking with habitus (of exclusion from rights) and embodying new habits, thereby transforming subjects into claimants of rights. This way citizenship is conceptualised beyond the principle of national sovereignty and becomes a terrain of struggle, a contested institution that non-citizens uproot through 'the plethora of political practices through which (they) make claims to belonging, inclusion and recognition in their societies of residence' (Swerts 2014, 297).

Rigo (2010) defines acts of *illegal* citizenship as those forms of mobilisation that instead of reinforcing state-centred notions of citizenship shift the focus to 'the ruptures and contradictions that these inflict upon the institutional definition and codification of citizenship' (200). This way, those who are formally excluded from citizenship, and as such from the right to have rights, subvert the field of politics by expanding its boundaries. A conceptualisation of *citizenship from below* (Nyers and Rygiel 2012), as opposed to the citizenship granted from the state, sees these struggles as transformative in challenging borders of political community, membership and notions of political subjectivity. Therefore, despite being denied of the formal enfranchisement to rights, undocumented migrants are capable to forge and express new political subjectivities, while challenging the politics and boundaries of citizenship.

Yet, criticism to this approach argued that enacting citizenship entails the expansion rather than the subversion of the borders, as a politics of inclusion risks reproducing racialised hierarchies of differential inclusion (Mezzadra and Neilson 2013). These critiques highlight four cardinal limitations of citizenship. Firstly, as citizenship is bound up with the Western nation-state and the capitalist politics of operations (Mezzadra and Neilson 2019), it is configured to be a device of differential inclusion and hierarchisation (McNevin 2011; Mezzadra and Neilson 2013). Secondly, as citizenship is designed as a biopolitical technology of control and subjection, it curtails mobility while institutionalising uncertainty and threats of deportability (Balibar 2009; De Genova 2016). Thirdly, citizenship cannot be assumed as the universally desired achievement and tool of liberation of migrants' mobilisations (Van Isacker 2019; Stojić Mitrović and Vilenica 2019). Lastly, citizenship is seen as a constraining framework, whereas governmental and humanitarian logic assume that non-citizens are devoid of voice and agency (Raimondi 2019).

Embracing the above criticism to the politics of citizenship, most contributions to this special issue propose different angles of analysis and empirical inquiry of those struggles that exceed the framework of citizenship and counter the politics of borders and their operation at the level of everyday lives. Indeed, the special issue is informed by the acknowledgement that the *acts of citizenship* approach relies on an understanding of resistance that is rooted in institutional politics and state regulation, which emphasises integration as a form of empowerment. Moreover, it might overshadow those struggles that refuse to engage in political demands as well as to pose claims for recognition to the state.

Following these lines of inquiry the following sections address the main bodies of knowledge informing the contributions to this special issue. The first part elaborates upon the *autonomy of migration* perspective, whose concepts are central to the overall approach of the special issue. We then move on to problematising the relation between inhabitance and citizenship. Inhabitance is configured as a constitutive process to opt out of the constraints determined by border management and the institutionalisation within the reception system. As such, inhabitance becomes a liberatory practice enacted through everyday life as well as contentious politics. This contesting function of inhabitance is even more apparent whenever the field of tensions between settlement and mobility leads to squats and other autonomous forms of settlement as the ones described within this special issue. These transformed, re-appropriated spaces become sites for contesting the restriction of mobility as well as for affirming migrants' *rightful presence* (Squire and Darling 2013). As such, they might become sites of the commoning (Linebaugh 2008) where urban and mobile commons (Papadopoulos and Tsianos 2013) are generated. Lastly, the conclusive section outlines the single contributions contained in the special issue.

The autonomy of migration

As argued above, the autonomy of migration approach contends that citizenship, whether formalised or performed, granted or enacted, is intertwined with sovereign governmentality, and not merely subjected to it (see Papadopoulos, Stephenson, and Tsianos 2008; Mudu and Chattopadhyay 2017). Following a Foucauldian understanding of the mutual relations between power and resistance, the *autonomy of migration* approach places resistance first: instead of looking at migration as a response to control and market forces, the autonomy of migration sees control as a reaction to migration, as an attempt to subject and discipline free movement through violence and repression. Here, so-called *border-work* figures as a contested process in continuous transformation, constantly redefined and shaped by those forces that attempt to escape controls (Mezzadra and Neilson 2013; Walters 2015). The novelty of this approach is to shift the focus from migration as a marginal reaction to the centrality of political and economic structures, to conceptualise it as a constituent force that actively defines political and social structures (Karakayali and Tsianos 2005; Papadopoulos, Stephenson and Tsianos 2008; Mezzadra 2010).

Consequently, this approach conceives border as an analytical lens that uncovers the multifarious fields of tensions, processes of subjectivation and politics unravelling in the act of contesting and crossing borders (Mezzadra and Neilson 2013). The border is indeed interpreted as an epistemological device, as a *method* (ibid.) to highlight the continuous redefinition of power relations by the conflicts between border governance and migrants' attempts to practice movement as well as settlement (Papadopoulos and Tsianos 2013). In this light, borders cannot be pictured as a fixed line of exclusion, in the same way as citizenship cannot be conceived as a 'static' snapshot of a supposedly socially and geographically discrete society which bestows a series of rights to the formally-defined citizen (Butler and Spivak 2007). In contrast, borders are interpreted as porous and flexible tools that are proliferating and moving from recognised borderlands to multifarious spatial scales, in response and reaction to migrants' movements and defiance.

Through this approach, traditional definitions of political action and mobilisation are contested. Instead of defining migrants' movements as actors who become political through demands for rights, inclusion and recognition, the *autonomy of migration* sees mobility and illegalised border crossing as political movements that escape state institutions and delegitimize sovereign control. This shifts away from politics concerned with the realm of citizenship-related rights, and instead highlights those horizontal practices, experiences and modes of contestation that circulate through borders, as well as the strategies and tactics that groups of migrants mobilise in their everyday encounters with border controls and security technologies (Papadopoulos et al. 2008).

The theoretical implications of this approach lead us to focus on how institutional politics is overwhelmed by autonomous forms of mobilisation, beyond and against the state and other forms of governance. Within this special issue, the autonomy of migration approach is therefore cardinal to the construction of a critical theory of citizenship and borders and it functions as an interpretative framework for practices of inhabitance through the commoning of everyday life and the establishment of solidarity networks. *Mobile commons* are largely accounted for as 'a world of knowledge, of information, of tricks for survival, of mutual care, of social relations, of services exchange, of solidarity and sociability' (Papadopoulos and Tsianos 2013, 190). Within this panoply of possibilities, housing squats (as City Plaza in Athens, We Are Here in Amsterdam, 4 Stelle Occupato in Rome and Ohlauer Strasse 12 in Berlin) can represent one of the possible materialisations of the mobile commons in the guise of invention, experimentation and multiplication of different practices and modes of life.

While the autonomy of migration perspective points at the constitution of *mobile commons* as on the move, precarious and ephemeral cracks and ruptures to bordering regimes, we argue that the forms of commoning produced in migrants' squats consolidate into forms of liberation that are not temporary or ephemeral. Under subjective, political and organisational circumstances unravelling in specific temporal and spatial arrangements, they may become durable and tangible infrastructures that can support people's efforts to move and settle according to their needs and aspirations, as well as spaces for expression of imperceptible politics (Linebaugh 2014). As such, inhabitance as a process of home-making can constitute a site of construction, maintenance and proliferation of mobile commons, inside and against borderlands, and beyond citizenship.

Inhabitance beyond citizenship

Following Lefebvre's articulation of *habitat* and *inhabitance,* we seek to draw parallels to current debates on the distinction between housing and home. In doing so, we address the practices of home-making in migrants' squats as an alternative to *being-housed*, as the pathways of citizenship and migration reception systems would prescribe. On the other hand, we propose the notion of inhabitance as a commoning practice that transgresses and subverts humanitarian and institutional attempts of housing people within emergency shelters and camps, as well as a practice that exceeds the politics of rights and citizenship.

This contrast uncovers the ambivalence of the notion of *home*. In the context of the bordering of Europe, *home* is often conflated with the individual's native state, hence with the nation and its identity politics, shaped around a racialised construction of otherness (Blunt and Dowling 2006). Moreover, often infused with naturalised gendered norms about heterosexual marriage and private life, home has often been addressed as in opposition to capitalism, rather than necessary to the reproduction of capitalist and patriarchal relations (Federici 2012). Doreen Massey (2013) critiques (mostly male) conceptualisations of home as a romantic, private and sacred space of safety and belonging. From this perspective, home is inevitably experienced as an enclosed site, a cage, where patriarchal violence, state morality and exploitative relations of production and reproduction are enforced (Fortier 2001; Wilkinson and Ortega-Alc àzar 2017). Besides, in a neoliberal context home-making is conflated with the individualised access to marketised housing through indebtedness, or to residual (and often stigmatised) social-welfare based housing (Martin 2002; Lazzarato 2012). Neoliberal individualised housing models turned homes into commodities subject to marketisation and dispossession (Madden and Marcuse 2016). Home, therefore, is a porous place that is neither private nor public, but is constituted at the intersections between the domestic and political worlds (Massey 2013; Blunt and Dowling 2006) and it constitutes a spatial and political technology of government of the population.

Looking at the material manifestations of home in relation to migration, housing provision for migrants produces and reproduces forms of subjection, spatial segregation and racial discrimination. State-run shelters and humanitarian camps engender a provision of home that is not oriented towards the satisfaction of needs, but rather prioritises forms of custody and containment through strict forms of control. These forms of governance do not only materialise through the securitised architecture of these spaces, such as fences, razor-wires, guards and observation points. They extend to biopolitical forms of care and to devices that order, schedule and confine migrants' bodies and everyday lives, according to minimum standards for survival (Agier 2011; Weizman 2011).

These policies fix migrants in temporal and spatial limbos, confining their possibilities of taking control over their lives and to make homes in displacement (Brun and Fábos 2015). According to Iris Marion Young, the notion of 'home as a critical value', minimal shelter prevents the possibility to exercise agency, as well as 'the development of the spirit of resistance' (Young 2005, 45). Following Young, Brun (2015), argues that migrants 'are often assigned to shelters that make people survive, but that cannot be transformed into home –they are shelters representing the interstices in displaced people's lives; no one is expected to stay there long, but rather to return home or move on' (ibid: 47). As these interstices unfold temporally and isolate them spatially, migrants experience the mixture between institutionalised boredom and the helplessness of waiting for their position of being *stuck* to be altered. Here, housing is a device to keep people *in their place*, thereby reinforcing the racist and patriarchal functions of home.

Rather than creating homes and forms of inhabitance, these politics produce *habitats*, namely containers of *habits* and social behavior through 'manipulating their environments' (Burgess 2012, 3). Habitat is here intended as a spatial technology of discipline and governmentality of *habits*, where racialised, classed, gendered and colonised populations are subject to 'a reinforcement of the disciplinary rigors of habit as the only effective means of guiding conduct' (Bennett et al. 2013, 6). However, following the work of Sullivan (2006), Carolyn Pedwell argues that the notion of habit contains an ambivalence, as it can engender both *stasis* and transformative practices: 'on the one hand, *habit* conjures unthinking reflex, mindless repetition, and hence *stasis*. Yet, on the other hand, without the formation of enduring habits, no substantive embodied, social or political change can take shape, and become rooted enough to sustain' (Pedwell 2017, 12). The question that follows, therefore, is how to produce liberating, rather than disciplining habits and habitats? In the next section we discuss the practice of home-making in migrants' squats as an attempt to subvert and transform the spatial technologies of *habitat* and *being housed* thereby producing forms of inhabitance that counter *stasis*, the state and its politics of citizenship.

Squatting, home-making and inhabitance

As opposed to the association of home to a patriarchal cage and prison, for post-colonial feminist scholars home can also be envisioned as a space for solidarity and resistance against oppression, slavery and racism (Collins 2002; hooks 1992; Young 2005). Blunt and Dowling's 'critical geography of home' (2006) places attention to the practice of home-making as a relational process and lived space continually created through everyday socio-political practices. They distinguish between housing as dwelling and *home*, where the latter is constituted by the relation between the material and the affective. They depict home as a 'spatial imaginary' and as a politicised process of both oppression and resistance: 'as spatialized feelings of belonging *and* alienation, desire *and* fear' they argue, 'the spatialities of home are broader and more complex than just housing' (10) and 'can be conceptualized as processes of establishing connections with others and creating a sense of belonging as part of rather than separate from society' (14).

Brun and Fábos (2015) discuss the multiple 'constellations of home' constituted by displaced migrants. They characterise home as a day-to-day practice as well as an affective space, while differentiating it from nationalist politics that construct exclusionary notions of homeland. As opposed to state policies and humanitarian practices that house migrants, Brun and Fabos refer to *making home* as the ways in which 'people try to gain control over their lives and (which) involves negotiating specific understandings of home, particular regimes of control and assistance, and specific locations and material structures' (ibid, 14). While the forms of control and immobility of the camp fix people into a static mode, they argue that the practices of making home engender forms of liminality, possibilities of movement, transgression, and transformation.

Following these discussions this special issue addresses the practice of home-making in migrants' squats as an alternative to *being housed*, thereby creating forms of inhabitance as opposed to being contained through *habitat*. Home is here conceptualised differently to the traditional domestic site, as it is instead a political and contested space constituted through relational and affective practices (Mohanty 2003; Ahmed 1999; Fortier 2001). Similarly, home-making is here addressed for its possibilities to engender commoning processes across which spaces are produced through scales of organisational, affective, political and social relations. The latter connect and hybridise with surrounding ecologies, subjectivities and infrastructures (Cooper 1986; Haraway 1991; Grazioli 2018).

The occupation of space is a well-established protest repertoire of urban movements across Europe. Over various decades, across a multiplicity of cities, squatters' movements have occupied vacant buildings and have created spaces for autonomy and self-organisation. Squatting is a form of direct action that is inseparable from housing struggles, where rent strikes, squatting, alternative planning and anti-eviction activism are the major forms of resistance to the relation between the hyper-commodification of housing, gentrification and intersectional injustices across class, gender and ethnic lines (Madden and Marcuse 2016).

In particular, the occupation of vacant buildings enables the satisfaction of immediate materials needs such as housing, as well as the provision of self-managed spaces for political organisation. While migrant squatters might engage in rights-claiming campaigns, a more significant feature of their politics is their immediate appropriation of spaces and infrastructures to foster their autonomous organisation. These practices engender resistance to a multiplicity of forms of hegemony and governmentality embroiled in everyday social reproduction. As squatting and informal settlements imply a process of construction of space and self-management of everyday life, they are increasingly included into debates around those political, relational, spatial processes that enable the commoning (Linebaugh 2008). As Montagna and Grazioli point out in their contribution, the burgeoning debate about *commoning* deflects the emphasis from the ownership and formal entitlement to the commons, in order to point out those human needs and radical infrastructures that are demanded within a post-capitalist, post-crisis world (Gibson-Graham 2006; Cattaneo and Martínez 2014). Besides, squatting as a direct act of spatial repossession allows manifold experimentation in the *here and now* of grassroots forms of governance based on solidarity, where new subjectivities are constituted (Dadusc 2019; Raimondi 2019).

According to this reflection, the contributions to this special issue address squats and informal settlement as spaces where migrants re-appropriate and resignify saturated and contested spaces, while experimenting modalities of everyday social reproduction that are alternative to capitalist ones (Gibson-Graham 2006; Linebaugh 2008). This includes contesting the spatialised housing segregation produced by racialised border regimes which curtail migrants' access to welfare-based provisions in neoliberal policies, and which force them into institutionalised housing (i.e. reception centres), camps, marginalised slums, or even detention centres.

Martínez (2017) distinguished four categories of migrants' involvement in squatting in the city of Madrid: autonomy, solidarity, engagement, and empowerment. Migrants can occupy buildings without the support of non-migrant local squatters. Sometimes a mutual cooperation between both groups is established. This can lead either to keep separate buildings for migrants and non-migrants, or to merge in the same buildings. Migrants can also join squats which were initiated by non-migrants usually according to the political traditions of squatting in the locality. The more cooperation occurs, the more likely is for migrants to be empowered and to incorporate squatting in their repertoire of action, survival, and political affirmation. Several activists and scholars (Dadusc 2017; Makrygianni 2017; García and Jørgensen 2019) emphasise the tensions that may arise between the autonomous initiatives of migrants and the solidarity they enjoy when native non-migrant people, with more or less background in squatting, become engaged. In short, the citizenship status and the strength of social networks create structural differences between migrant and native squatters, although a long-lasting anti-racist and anti-fascist stance in left-libertarian milieus helps to ease solidarity and cooperation in this matter.

Migrants have joined housing movements and organisations such as Droit Au Logement (DAL) in France (Aguilera 2018), Coordinamento Cittadino di Lotta per la Casa (CCLC) and Blocchi Precari Metropolitani (BPM) in Italy (Grazioli and Caciagli 2018), or the Plataforma de Afectados por la Hipoteca (PAH) in Spain (Martínez 2018). Although from the perspective of the 'deprivation' approach there would be a tendency to demand state-backed access to housing or the legalisation of the squats (usually, in terms of affordable rental contracts) promoted by these housing groups, these struggles have also politicised and radicalised housing issues beyond the limited scope of some autonomist networks of squatters. Some remarkable examples, such as Metropoliz in Rome (Grazioli and Caciagli 2018) and City Plaza in Athens (García and Jørgensen 2019; Raimondi, 2019) have shown that strong and horizontal forms of self-management of the squats are not only possible, but also foster intersectional everyday politics as well as forms of mobilisation where diverse social and political struggles can converge. Although each squatted space is ephemeral, precarious or uncertain, the forms of commoning created in these spaces survive the eviction of each individual squat, and multiply beyond its walls. Their peculiarity is that they do not only form momentary ruptures to the sovereign filtering of mobility. Rather than mere episodes or events that disrupt habit they produce alternative habitats and forms of inhabitance, through the practice of space-making and home-making. Through squatting migrants do not only perform resistance in the sense of opposition and reaction to bordering regimes, but organise their lives differently, as to counter and escape economic, social and political subjection.

There is always a dialectical relation between the enclosures and the opening of new possibilities of commoning and resistance. The enclosure of these forms of commoning is performed through repression and erasure (Van Isacker 2019), through humanitarian interventions (Dadusc 2019), through rights and laws (Montagna and Grazioli 2019), through forced circulation (Stojić Mitrović and Vilenica 2019) as well as through what Sara Ahmed (2014) defines *atmospheric walls*, namely visible and invisible techniques and micropolitics that inevitably make spaces available to some more than to others.

Indeed, squats are far from romantic ideas of harmonious communities, as they engender tensions, conflicts and contradictions (see Raimondi 2019). As Julia Downes (forthcoming) argues, grassroots movements 'are not immune from perpetuating systems of domination; however, we can work towards attending to power inequalities that emerge in our interventions'. These spaces do not attempt to provide blueprints and solutions to fix all the problems created by global inequality, but engender attempts and failures, learning from mistakes, facing internalised forms of racism and privilege: *Caminando preguntamos* (as we walk, we ask questions).

Towards a politics of inhabitance

Following the lead of these main conceptual threads, the contributions presented in the following and final section develop critical perspectives rooted in the materiality of migrants' struggles within European borderlands. This empirical approach is nurtured by the authors' activist participation into the fieldwork (Juris and Khasnabish 2013; Dadusc 2014). Indeed, the editors' and authors' shared perspectives, which shaped the special issue, is that activist researchers "must always stress the inseparability of knowledge and action, which impel them to be self-consciously interventionist in approach' (Routledge 2013, 267).

Marta Stojić Mitrović and Ana Vilenica look at the migrants' struggles about housing in Serbia in the context of the securitisation policies that characterise the EU's external *borderscapes* of Serbia. The Western Balkans, they argue, became not only transit spaces, but also *circular transit* spaces where migrants are forced to cross borders endlessly without moving forward to their destination. The authors propose the notion of 'housingscapes' to address those practices that emerge from mobile spatialities and vulnerabilities. In particular, they point to the intersections of state-run camps and migrant self-organised squatted housing. Squatting initiatives have taken place along the main migratory routes, crossroads and borders, but also next to the state-run camps and even within them. Therefore, Stojić Mitrović and Vilenica show how these housing infrastructures constitute practices of commoning and of 'debordering circulation', which imply a confrontation and transformation of the border regimes forced circulation.

Valeria Raimondi's article analyses the socio-political form of the migrants' squats, the (new) subjectivities they contribute to create, and the socio-spatial interactions they foster and generate, both within them and in relation to other spatialities in the city of Athens. The implementation of the analysis happens at different spatial scales – from the intimate scale of the body to the wider one of the city. Theoretically, the article develops along the lines of three concepts: citizenship, space and autonomy. Migrants' squats are interpreted here as practices and sites for contesting citizenship, intended as a category of political status; as such, they exceed the limits of this category and move beyond the boundaries of the nation-state, originating practices of citizenship 'from below' (Nyers and Rygiel 2012), while at the same time they produce subjectivities that choose to *opt out* of citizenship as legal status (McNevin 2013).

Nicola Montagna and Margherita Grazioli's paper examines the case of Rome (Italy), where the linkage between migration, urban planning and self-management has been constitutive of the urban fabric since the end of WWII. As the 2000s so-called 'migratory crisis' unfolded, thousand of migrants with different statuses and migratory trajectories settled, transited or got forcibly 'stuck' in Rome. Grassroots forms of inhabitance, including housing squats, urban camps and informal settlement, represented a viable alternative to the institutional reception system, and for opting out the pathways established by the Dublin border regime. The interplay of autonomy and coercion underpinning these forms of self-made inhabitance situates the ontological conditions of possibility under which they can be constituted, and maintained, as urban and mobile commons (Papadopoulos and Tsianos 2013). The latter are understood as those organisational, relational and political deeds which foster migrants' settlement and mobility. The potentiality, and odds, of self-made inhabitance as urban-mobile commons are discussed through three case-studies: the housing squat '4 Stelle Occupato', affiliated to Housing Rights Movements; the urban camping Baobab Experience; and the informal settlement Ex-Penicillina Leo.

Deanna Dadusc's paper addresses the autonomous forms of inhabitance of We are here grassroots movement in the inner EU borderland of the Netherlands. According to the author, the creation of housing squats, as opposed to the containment in emergency shelters, marks an important shift in migrants' struggles that goes from acts of protest, to the performance of resistance at the level of the micropolitics of borders. Through these spaces, indeed *illegalised* migrants enact presence without necessarily conflating with, or demanding, citizenship. Moreover, focussing on government's responses to these forms of inhabitance, the paper uncovers the simultaneously humanitarian and securitarian nature of border regimes.

Travis van Isacker's contribution addresses the iterated eviction and dismantlement of Calais' unauthorised camps and squats as domicide (Porteous and Smith 2001) and as a technology of citizenship. Here, *domicide* qualifies as the deliberate destruction of autonomous forms of inhabitance. The clearance of these spaces through forcible evictions and displacement operates as a technology of citizenship in two main ways: prescribing politically acceptable forms of inhabitance by dismantling others, and physically removing sites of contestation where networks of solidarity and politics of anti-citizenship are nurtured. This politics of exhaustion is read as an attempt to implement citizenship as a device of control of settlement and mobility.

De Angelis' postface addresses the above papers and proposes an understanding of commoning as an ongoing flow constituent of rights that are enacted and exercised, rather than being *granted* by the state. In particular, De Angelis explores the relation between commoning, enclosure and citizenship and argues that the common is a pre-condition for citizenship and it exceeds its constraints: 'in the here and now, in the daily challenge of migrants' social reproduction, commoning emerges as a way to facilitate existence while increasing the power of resistance' (De Angelis 2019, 635). In this context, besides a multiplicity of attempts to enclose bodies, lives and spaces, these struggles become increasingly ungovernable.

Note

1. https://alarmphone.org/en/2018/06/17/toward-a-coalition-of-solidarity-for-the-right-to-mobility-and-equal-rights-for-all/ .

Acknowlegments

We wish to acknowledge Nina Fraeser, Eleni Dimou and the Feminist Autonomous Centre for Research (Athens) for their precious support, insight and comments on the arguments of this special issue; Vaso Makrygianni for proposing the notion of inhabitance as a valuable perspective to discuss migrants' occupations; all the anonymous reviewers for their supportive feedback and invaluable work on each paper of this special issue.

Disclosure statement

No potential conflict of interest was reported by the authors.

ORCID

Miguel A. Martínez ⓘ http://orcid.org/0000-0001-5511-2390

References

Aas, K. F. 2011. "Crimmigrant'bodies and Bona Fide Travelers: Surveillance, Citizenship and Global Governance." *Theoretical Criminology* 15 (3): 331–346. doi:10.1177/1362480610396643.

Agamben, G. 1998. *Homo Sacer: Sovereign Power and Bare Life*. Palo Alto: Stanford University Press.

Agier, M. 2011. *Managing the Undesirables*. Cambridge: Polity.

Aguilera, T. 2018. "The Squatting Movement (S) in Paris: Internal Divides and Conditions for Survival." In *The Urban Politics of Squatters' Movements*, edited by Miguel A. Martínez, 121–144. New York: Palgrave Macmillan.

Ahmed, S. 1999. "Home and Away: Narratives of Migration and Estrangement." *International Journal of Cultural Studies* 2 (3): 329–347. doi:10.1177/136787799900200303.

Ahmed, S. 2014. *Willful Subjects*. Durham: Duke University Press.

Anderson, B., N. Sharma, and C. Wright. 2009. "Why No Borders?" *Refuge: Canada's Journal on Refugees* 26 (2): 5–18.

Arendt, H. 1973. *The Origins of Totalitarianism*. Vol. 348. Boston: Houghton Mifflin Harcourt.

Ataç, I., K. Rygiel, and M. Stierl. 2016. "Introduction: The Contentious Politics of Refugee and Migrant Protest and Solidarity Movements: Remaking Citizenship from the Margins." *Citizenship Studies* 20 (5): 527–544. doi:10.1080/13621025.2016.1182681.

Attoh, K. A. 2011. ""What *Kind* of Right Is the Right to the City?"." *Human Geography* 35 (5): 669–685. doi:10.1177/0309132510394706.

Balibar, E. 2009. *We, the People of Europe?: Reflections on Transnational Citizenship.* Princeton: Princeton University Press.

Bennett, T., F. Dodsworth, G. Noble, M. Poovey, and M. Watkins. 2013. "Habit and Habituation: Governance and the Social." *Body & Society* 19 (2): 3–29. doi:10.1177/1357034X13485881.

Blunt, A., and R. M. Dowling. 2006. *Home.* Abingdon: Routledge.

Bosworth, M., and M. Guild. 2008. "Governing through Migration Control: Security and Citizenship in Britain." *The British Journal of Criminology* 48 (6): 703–719. doi:10.1093/bjc/azn059.

Bowling, B. 2013. "Epilogue: The Borders of Punishment: Towards a Criminology of Mobility." In *The Borders of Punishment: Migration, Citizenship, and Social Exclusion*, edited by K. F. Aas and M. Bosworth, 291–306. Oxford: Oxford University Press.

Brun, C. 2015. "Active Waiting and Changing Hopes: Toward a Time Perspective on Protracted Displacement." *Social Analysis* 59 (1): 19–37. doi:10.3167/sa.2015.590102.

Brun, C., and A. Fábos. 2015. "Making Homes in Limbo? A Conceptual Framework." *Refuge: Canada's Journal on Refugees* 31 (1): 5–17.

Burgess, A. 2012. "'Nudging'healthy Lifestyles: The UK Experiments with the Behavioural Alternative to Regulation and the Market." *European Journal of Risk Regulation* 3 (1): 3–16. doi:10.1017/S1867299X00001756.

Butler, J., and G. C. Spivak. 2007. *Who Sings the Nation-State?: Language, Politics, Belonging.* Kolkata: Seagull Books.

Carr, M. 2015. *Fortress Europe. Inside the War against Immigration.* London: Jurst&Company.

Casas-Cortes, M., S. Cobarrubias, N. De Genova, G. Garelli, G. Grappi, C. Heller, S. Hess, et al. 2015. "New Keywords: Migration and Borders." *Cultural Studies* 29 (1): 55–87. doi:10.1080/09502386.2014.891630.

Cattaneo, C., and M. A. Martínez. 2014. "Squatting as an Alternative to Capitalism: An Introduction." In *Squatters' Movement in Europe: Commons and Autonomy as Alternatives to Capitalism*, edited by Squatting Europe Kollective, 1–23. London: Pluto Press.

Collins, P. H. 2002. *Black Feminist Thought: Knowledge, Consciousness, and the Politics of Empowerment.* London: Routledge.

Cooper, R. 1986. "Organization/disorganization." *Social Science Information* 25 (2): 299–335. doi:10.1177/053901886025002001.

Dadusc, D. 2014. "Power, Knowledge, and Resistances in the Study of Social Movements." *Contention* 1 (2): 48–60.

Dadusc, D. 2017. ""Squatting and the Undocumented Migrants' Struggle in the Netherlands." Chapter 22. In *Migration, Squatting and Radical Autonomy*, edited by P. Mudu and S. Chattopadhyay, New York: Routledge.

Dadusc, D. 2019a. "Enclosing Autonomy: The Politics of Tolerance and Criminalisation of Squatting." *City* 23 (2): 170–188. doi:10.1080/13604813.2019.1615760.

Dadusc, D. 2019b. "The Micropolitics of Border Struggles." *Citizenship Studies* 23 (6).

Dadusc, D., and P. Mudu. 2019 – forthcoming. ""Care without Control" - the Humanitarian Industrial Complex and the Criminalisation of Migrants Solidarity." *Geopolitics.*

De Angelis, M. 2019. "Migrants' Inhabiting through Commoning and State Enclosures. A Postface." *Citizenship Studies* 23 (6).

De Genova, N. 2016. "Detention, Deportation, and Waiting: Toward a Theory of Migrant Detainability." *Global Detention Project* Working Paper No. 18. https://www.globaldetention project.org/wp-content/uploads/2016/12/De-Genova-GDP-Paper-2016.pdf

De Souza, M. L. 2010. "Which Right to Which City? in Defence of Political-Strategic Clarity." *Interface* 2 (1): 315–333.

Dikeç, M. 2013. "Immigrants, Banlieues, and Dangerous Things: Ideology as an Aesthetic Affair." *Antipode* 45 (1): 23–42. doi:10.1111/anti.2013.45.issue-1.

Downes, J. forthcoming. "Re-Imagining an End to Gendered Violence: Prefiguring the Worlds We Want." In *Resisting the Punitive State: Theory, Practice, Struggle and Action*, edited by J. Greener, E. Hart, and R. Moth. London: Pluto Press.

Elden, S. 2004. "Between Marx and Heidegger: Politics, Philosophy and Lefebvre's the Production of Space." *Antipode* 36 (1): 86–105. doi:10.1111/anti.2004.36.issue-1.

Fassin, D. 2011. *Humanitarian Reason: A Moral History of the Present*. Oakland: University of California Press.

Federici, S. 2012. *Revolution at Point Zero: Housework, Reproduction, and Feminist Struggle*. Oakland: PM press.

Fortier, A. 2001. "'Coming Home' Queer Migrations and Multiple Evocations of Home." *European Journal of Cultural Studies* 4 (4): 405–424. doi:10.1177/136754940100400403.

García, A. O., and M. B. Jørgensen. 2019. "Autonomous Solidarity: Hotel City Plaza." In *Solidarity and the'Refugee Crisis' in Europe*, edited by A. O. García and M. B. Jørgensen, 49–72. Cham: Palgrave Pivot.

Garelli, G., and M. Tazzioli. 2018. "The Humanitarian War against Migrant Smugglers at Sea." *Antipode* 50 (3): 685–703. doi:10.1111/anti.2018.50.issue-3.

Geddes, A. 2001. "Immigration and European Integration: Towards Fortress Europe?" *Refugee Survey Quarterly* 20 (1): 229–229.

Gibson-Graham, J. K. 2006. *A Postcapitalist Politics*. Minneapolis, MN: University of Minnesota Press.

Grazioli, M. 2018. "*The 'Right to the City' in the Post-Welfare Metropolis. Community-Building, Autonomous Infrastructures and Urban Commons in Rome's Self-Organised Housing Squats*". PhD Thesis, University of Leicester.

Grazioli, M., and C. Caciagli. 2018. "Resisting to the Neoliberal Urban Fabric: Housing Rights Movements and the Re-Appropriation of the 'Right to the City' in Rome, Italy." *Voluntas 1* 29 (4): 697–711.

Grazioli, M., and N. Montagna. 2019. "Urban Commons and Freedom of movement: The Housing Struggles of Recently Arrived Migrants and Refugees in Rome." *Citizenship Studies* 23 (6).

Haraway, D. 1991. *Simians, Cyborgs and Women: The Reinvention of Nature*. London: Routledge.

Harvey, D. 2012. *Rebel Cities. From the Right to the City to the Urban Revolution*. London: Verso.

Hodkinson, S. 2012. "The Return of the Housing Question." *Ephemera: Theory & Politics in Organization* 12 (4): 423–444.

Hodkinson, S., and P. Chatterton. 2006. "Autonomy in the City? Reflections on the Social Centres Movement in the UK." *City* 10 (3): 305–315. doi:10.1080/13604810600982222.

hooks, B. 1992. *Representing Whiteness in the Black Imagination*. New York: Routledge.

Ikizoglu Erensu, A. 2016. "Notes from a Refugee Protest: Ambivalences of Resisting and Desiring Citizenship." *Citizenship Studies* 20 (5): 664–677. doi:10.1080/13621025.2016.1182677.

Isin, E. F., and G. M. Nielsen. 2008. "Introduction: Acts of Citizenship." In *Acts of Citizenship*, edited by E. F. Isin and G. M. Nielsen, 1–14. London: Zed Books.

Isin, E. F. 2008. "Theorizing Acts of Citizenship." In *Acts of Citizenship*, edited by E. F. Isin and G. M. Nielsen, 15–43. London: Zed Books.

Juris, J. S., and A. Khasnabish. 2013. *Insurgent Encounters. Transnational Activism, Ethnography and the Political*. Durham/London: Duke University Press.

Karakayali, S., and V. Tsianos. 2005. "Mapping the Order of New Migration. Undokumentierte Arbeit Und Die Autonomie Der Migration." *PERIPHERIE–Politik• Ökonomie• Kultur* 97/98: 35–64.

Lazzarato, M. 2012. *The Making of the Indebted Man: An Essay on the Neoliberal Condition*. Cambridge: MIT Press.

Lefebvre, H. 2003. *The Urban Revolution*. Minneapolis: University of Minnesota Press.

Linebaugh, P. 2008. *The Magna Carta Manifesto: Liberties and Commons for All*. Berkeley: University of California Press.

Linebaugh, P. 2014. *Stop, Thief!: The Commons, Enclosures, and Resistance*. San Francisco: PM Press.

Madden, D., and P. Marcuse. 2016. *In Defense of Housing*. London: Verso.

Maestri, G., and S. M. Hughes. 2017. "Contested Spaces of Citizenship: Camps, Borders and Urban Encounters." *Citizenship Studies* 21 (6): 625–639. doi:10.1080/13621025.2017.1341657.

Makrygianni, V. 2017. "Migrant Squatters in the Greek Territory. Practices of Resistance and the Production of the Athenian Urban Space." In *Migration, Squatting and Radical Autonomy*, edited by P. Mudu and S. Chattopadhyay, 248–256. New York: Routledge.

Martin, R. 2002. *Financialization of Daily Life*. Philadelphia: Temple University Press.

Martínez, M. A. 2017. "Squatters and Migrants in Madrid: Interactions, Contexts and Cycles." *Urban Studies* 54 (11): 2472–2489. doi:10.1177/0042098016639011.

Martínez, M. A. 2018. "Bitter Wins or a Long-Distance Race? Social and Political Outcomes of the Spanish Housing Movement." *Housing Studies*. https://www.tandfonline.com/doi/full/10.1080/02673037.2018.1447094.

Massey, D. 2013. *Space, Place and Gender*. Hoboken: John Wiley & Sons.

McNevin, A. 2011. *Contesting Citizenship: Irregular Migrants and New Frontiers of the Political*. New York: Columbia University Press.

McNevin, A. 2013. "Ambivalence and Citizenship: Theorising The Political Claims of Irregular Migrants." *Millennium* 41 (2): 182–200. doi:10.1177/0305829812463473.

Mezzadra, S. 2010. "The Gaze of Autonomy: Capitalism, Migration and Social Struggles." In *The Contested Politics of Mobility*, edited by V. Squire, 141–162. London: Routledge.

Mezzadra, S., and B. Neilson. 2013. *Border as Method, Or, the Multiplication of Labor*. Durham/London: Duke University Press.

Mezzadra, S., and B. Neilson. 2019. *The Politics of Operations. Excavating Contemporary Capitalism*. Durham/London: Duke University Press.

Mohanty, C. T. 2003. *Feminism without Borders*. Durham: Duke University Press.

Mudu, P., and S. Chattopadhyay. 2017. *Migration, Squatting and Radical Autonomy*. New York: Routledge.

Nicholls, W., and J. Uitermark. 2017. *Cities and Social Movements. Immigrant Rights Activism in the United States, France, and the Netherlands, 1970-2015*. Oxford: Wiley-Blackwell.

Nyers, P. 2015. "Migrant Citizenships and Autonomous Mobilities." *Migration, Mobility, & Displacement* 1 (1): 23–39. doi:10.18357/mmd11201513521.

Nyers, P., and K. Rygiel. 2012. *Citizenship, Migrant Activism and the Politics of Movement*. London: Routledge. doi:10.4324/9780203125113.

Pallister-Wilkins, P. 2017. "Humanitarian Borderwork." In *Border Politics*, edited by C. Günay and N. Witjespp, 85–103. Cham: Springer.

Pallister-Wilkins, P. 2018. "Hotspots and The Geographies Of Humanitarianism." *Environment and Planning D: Society and Space*. doi:10.1177/0263775818754884.

Papadopoulos, D., N. Stephenson, and V. Tsianos. 2008. *Escape Routes. Control and Subversion in the 21st Century*. London – Ann Arbor: MI: Pluto Press.

Papadopoulos, D., and V. Tsianos. 2013. "After Citizenship: Autonomy of Migration, Organisational Ontology and Mobile Commons." *Citizenship Studies* 17 (2): 178–196. doi:10.1080/13621025.2013.780736.

Pedwell, C. 2017. "Transforming Habit: Revolution, Routine and Social Change." *Cultural Studies* 31 (1): 93–120. doi:10.1080/09502386.2016.1206134.

Porteous, D., and S. E. Smith. 2001. *Domicide: The Global Destruction of Home*. Kingston: McGill-Queen's Press-MQUP.

Purcell, M. 2014. "Possible Worlds: Henri Lefebvre and the Right to the City." *Journal of Urban Affairs* 36 (1): 141–154. doi:10.1111/juaf.12034.

Raimondi, V. 2019. "'For Common Struggles of Migrants and Locals'. Experiences of Squatting between Local and Migrant Activists in Athens." *Citizenship Studies* 23 (6).

Rajaram, P. K., and C. Grundy-Warr, eds. 2007. *Borderscapes: Hidden Geographies and Politics at Territory's Edge*. Minneapolis: University of Minnesota Press.

Rajaram, P. K., and C. Grundy-Warr. 2004. "The Irregular Migrant as Homo Sacer: Migration and Detention in Australia, Malaysia, and Thailand." *International Migration* 42 (1): 33–64. doi:10.1111/imig.2004.42.issue-1.

Ramadan, A. 2013. "Spatialising the Refugee Camp." *Transactions of the Institute of British Geographers* 38 (1): 65–77. doi:10.1111/tran.2012.38.issue-1.

Rigo, E. 2010. "Citizens despite Borders: Challenges to the Territorial Order of Europe." In *The Contested of Mobility: Borderzones and Irregularity*, edited by V. Squire, 219–235. London: Routledge.

Rolnik, R. 2014. "Place, Inhabitance and Citizenship: The Right to Housing and the Right to the City in the Contemporary Urban World." *International Journal of Housing Policy* 14 (3): 293–300. doi:10.1080/14616718.2014.936178.

Routledge, P. 2013. "Activist Ethnography and Translocal Solidarity." In *Insurgent Encounters. Transnational Activism, Ethnography and the Political*, edited by S. Shukaitis and A. Khasnabish, 250–268. Durham/London: Duke University Press.

Salter, M. B. 2008. "When the Exception Becomes the Rule: Borders, Sovereignty, and Citizenship." *Citizenship Studies* 12 (4): 365–380. doi:10.1080/13621020802184234.

Simpson, L. 2011. *Dancing on Our Turtle's Back: Stories of Nishnaabeg Re-Creation, Resurgence and a New Emergence*. Winnipeg: Arbeiter Ring Press.

Squire, V., and J. Darling. 2013. "The "Minor" Politics of Rightful Presence: Justice and Relationality in City of Sanctuary." *International Political Sociology* 7 (1): 59–74. doi:10.1111/ips.2013.7.issue-1.

Stavrides, S. 2016. *Common Space. The City as Commons*. London: Zed Books.

Stierl, M. 2018. *Migrant Resistance in Contemporary Europe: Resistance as Method*. London: Routledge.

Stojic Mitrovic, M., and A. Vilenica. 2019. "Enforcing and Disrupting Circular Movement in an EU Borderscape: Housingscaping in Serbia." *Citizenship Studies* 23 (6).

Sullivan, S. 2006. *Revealing Whiteness: The Unconscious Habits of Racial Privilege*. Bloomington: Indiana University Press.

Swerts, T. 2014. "Non-Citizen Citizenship in Canada and the United States." In *Routledge Handbook of Global Citizenship Studies*, edited by E. F. Isin and P. Nyers, 295–303. London: Routledge.

Tazzioli, M. 2015. *Spaces of Governmentality: Autonomous Migration and the Arab Spring*. London: Rowman & Littlefield.

Ticktin, M. 2011. *Casualties of Care: Immigration and the Politics of Humanitarianism in France*. Oakland: University of California Press.

Van Isacker, T. 2019. "Bordering through Domicide: Spatializing Citizenship in Calais." *Citizenship Studies* 23 (6).

Vaughan-Williams, N. 2009. *Border Politics: The Limits of Sovereign Power: The Limits of Sovereign Power*. Edinburgh: Edinburgh University Press.

Walters, W. 2010. "Foucault and Frontiers: Notes on the Birth of the Humanitarian Border." In *Governmentality: Current Issues and Future Challenges*, edited by U. Bröckling, S. Krasmann, and T. Lemke, 146–172. London: Routledge.

Walters, W. 2015. "Reflections on Migration and Governmentality." *Movements. Journal for Critical Migration and Border Regime Studies* 1 (1): 1–25.

Weizman, E. 2011. *The Least of All Possible Evils: Humanitarian Violence from Arendt to Gaza*. London: Verso Books.

Wilkinson, E., and I. Ortega-Alcàzar. 2017. "A Home of One's Own? Housing Welfare for 'Young Adults' in Times of Austerity." *Critical Social Policy* 37 (3): 329–347. doi:10.1177/0261018317699804.

Young, I. M. 2005. *On Female Body Experience: Throwing like a Girl and Other Essays*. Oxford: Oxford University Press

Enforcing and disrupting circular movement in an EU Borderscape: housingscaping in Serbia

Marta Stojić Mitrović* and Ana Vilenica*

ABSTRACT

This article examines Western Balkans/EU bordering and debordering practices through a borderscape method in the context of the geopolitical positionality and (de)institutionalization of migrant housing in Serbia. From this perspective, a new 'border variation' can be seen emerging after the securitarian turn, transforming the external borderscape of the EU into a space of circular movement. The article sheds light on discourses, practices and places that constitute these spaces of circular movement within the EU external borderscape. In particular, the Western Balkans borderscape is investigated with reference to Serbian migrant housingscapes emerging at the intersection of state-run camps and migrant collective self-organized squatted housing. The focus on migrant housingscapes points to the interconnectedness of camps and squats in the process of facilitating circular movement by the state, the production of mobile commons as a debordering practice, and the production of visual representations of the external border as stabilized 'scape' for the EU.

Introduction

Transit migration in the Balkans came under the spotlight only recently in 2015, during the 'summer of migration' (Kasparek and Speer 2015). Images of people crossing 'green borders' between Western Balkans (WB) states,[1] lines of people walking on the rails or village roads, sleeping in the fields or city-parks flooded international media (The Boston Globe 2015; Daily Mail 2015; The Guardian 2015). The Balkan Route became a widespread topic of interest for a variety of professionals, journalists, researchers, activists, politicians, (inter)national security organizations and humanitarians. The publically shared photos and videos helped in building a distinctive imagery of the Route, as one of the epitomes of 'refugee/migrant crisis' (Arcimaviciene and Baglama 2018), even though multiple migrations have happened in this space over time. 'My grandmother also crossed this border between Serbia, then Yugoslavia, and Hungary, when she was going from Pakistan to UK', noted a former translator for an international humanitarian organization during our fieldwork in the border area in May 2018. 'I also encountered a travel book where the guy describes how he was hiding in a house in Horgos back in the 1960s', she added as we passed through the same

---

*These authors contributed equally to this work.

village in the northernmost part of Serbia on our way to the self-organized migrant settlement H2, as classified by non-governmental organizations (NGOs) that had been providing water, clean clothes, food and medical aid to migrants. The sudden visibility of the Balkans as a place of transit migrations is related to the production of 'the European refugee crisis' as a discursive frame (De Genova and Tazzioli 2016). The practices of migration, its facilitation and prevention are, on the other hand, shaped by geopolitical processes in the region, first and foremost the gradual integration of the Balkans, and especially its Western Balkan nation-states, into the European Union (EU) border regime, as building blocks of the external border of the EU.

The paternalistic, or neo-colonial, relation of the EU toward the 'failed states of the Balkans' (Musliu 2015, 371–373), which the EU offers to 'fix' by sets of direct and indirect political, administrative, technical and economic interventions, resulted in creation of a specific borderscape, constructed and contested dispositif[2] of the edge of a territory, where bordering practices take place (Rajaram and Grundy-Warr 2007, XXVIII). The concept of borderscape accentuates the social and political production of a border that ceases to be spatially limited, i.e., perceived as related to a physical territory. Instead, it is acknowledged as a complex and always fragmented arena of intertwined and juxtaposed socio-spatial agencies engaged in a dynamic struggle for dominance over manners and targets of exclusion/inclusion (Rajaram and Grundy-Warr 2007, XVI). This concept thus allows us to emphasize the epistemological, performative and communicational nature of the processes of both bordering, through which the divisions are established, and debordering, where previously established borders are ignored, confronted or erased. These processes are always done in specific settings, by specific actors, and for specific audiences. The Western Balkans is produced as a borderscape of the EU by and for the EU.

In this article, we will focus on two of the pervading internal discrepancies existing in the imaginary of the WB borderscape and Serbia in particular, namely the contested conceptualization of the borderscape as a space of transit or a space of containment, a space of movement control or a space of movement facilitation. We will follow how the increased impermeability of the borders of the EU and Schengen zone member-states that are surrounding WB resulted in the production of new types of (im)mobilities. Already the corridor going from northern Greece to southern Austria from October 2015 to March 2016 across several WB states had a distinctive securitarian-humanitarian nature, manifested in confinement of people in concentrated unidirectional transit mobility (Petrović 2016, 406; Hameršak and Pleše 2017, 9–41; Tazzioli 2018). Similarly, in the Greek hotspots, which function as another borderscape, people are free to travel throughout the islands, though not to the mainland or elsewhere (Tazzioli and Garelli 2018, 4). In the WB borderscape, following the closure of the corridor in March 2016, special mechanisms to govern people's mobility were put in place: multifaceted, multi-layered capturing of people in forced circular mobility, where people can move but on special routes, stretching across borders of Western Balkans nation-states that are carved within the struggle with ever more powerful humanitarian-securitarian regime.

In this article, we will analyse the internal discrepancies of the borderscaping processes in Serbia related to the spaces where migrants live. In particular, we will focus on two types of collective housing: state-run camps and migrant self-organized squats. The basic human need for shelter has become a symbol and a tool of bordering and debordering practices, a means through which people enter into social-economic-political-bordering relations, and negotiate their position. Unlike the notion of home, which emphasizes personal, familiar, private, domestic and, above all, inward-oriented aspect of dwelling, the notion of housing enables us to stress the contextual factors that influence it, as well as its public and outward-oriented communicational dimension, or, to put it differently, it enables us to see housing above all as an instrument of political confrontation (on difference between home and house see Boccagni and Brighenti 2017).

In the external borderscape, housing represents a domain of policing migration as well as of different struggles for free movement. We perceive camps and squats as topographical and topological elements (Giaccaria and Minca 2011) where agencies of both movement prevention and movement facilitation constantly intersect, resulting in the emergence of bordering and debordering practices through housing, or, in other words, in contested and negotiated housingscapes. We use the concept housingscape because it points that housing cannot be bounded to particular objects and spaces, but its rather fluid and amorphous spatiality renders it pliable and therefore readily subjected to manipulation. This manipulation is conducted by differently positioned actors in order to reach practical goals which often go far beyond both physical spaces and their nominal function of accommodation. To accentuate confronting agencies, processional, situational and temporal character of housingscapes, we use the gerund/participle form housingscaping. We consider this notion to be more suitable than camp-scape because the 'scape' of housing goes beyond camps and their spatial thresholds (Giaccaria and Minca 2011) and 'misery belts' (Martin 2015, 12–13) into different enactments of housing that relate to each other, inform and eat into each other (Jagetic Andersen and Pedersen 2018, 83).

The research presented here is a part of ongoing research on migration processes in Serbia and the region, starting in early 2012, based on three major types of material. The first is collected from written sources, in particular national and international legislation, reports produced and published by international, state and civil sector organizations and commissions, public statements of politicians and practitioners from the field of migration, as well as the material gathered from mainstream and social media. The second type of material is from observations and conversations obtained during multi-sited ethnographic fieldworks conducted in various locations in Serbia. Throughout the period, we conducted interviews with migrants, activists, members of the local population and professionals from the state and the civil sectors. Besides participation in public debates and expert meetings of practitioners, we have also been involved in activities of migrant solidarity networks in the region. All the material from interviews has been anonymized.

The material is presented in three sections focusing on the integration of Serbia as a Western Balkans state into the European border regime, the forced circular mobility within the borderscape, and the migrant housingscapes. With each, we try to follow the diachronic line in order to capture the dynamic features of borderscaping practices.

Serbia: constructing the external borderscape of the EU

The policy of externalization of the EU migration control to non-EU states is not a new phenomenon. In fact, this program has existed for more than two decades (Collinson 1996; Lavenex 1999; Papadopoulou-Kourkoula 2008). At first, the concept and policy decision of using 'surrounding states to protect the core of the EU from unwanted migration' (Thouez 2000) was not directly articulated, out of fear of (anti)colonial and (anti)elitist debates, but stayed in the background of numerous developmental projects, trade treaties, security deals, etc. Further, some authors avoid the concept of 'externalization' itself, as it implied asymmetrical power positions of the parties involved. Instead of the term externalization of borders, they tend to choose 'external dimension of the EU policy', since it conceals this asymmetry by assigning the emphasis on the cooperation of the EU with regional non-EU partners (Papadopoulou-Kourkoula 2008, 32). Beneath those euphemisms lies the interest of the European imperial and neo-colonial attempts to filter the flow of migrants by imposing operations of security and control to the territories from which the migrants come or pass through.

Borderscape is a useful concept that has already been employed to describe the process of externalization of the EU borders (Brambilla 2015). The term borderscape emphasizes plural, dynamic, relational, contested and de-territorialized aspects of socio-spatial agencies of ordering and exclusion that evade nation-state territorialities. Borderscapes are spaces of interaction between state and capital and a place of complex tensions that produce institutionalization and de-institutionalization of borders. By using borderscapes as a methodological angle, Chiara Brambilla (Ibid.) has described post-colonial scenarios of externalization of EU borders overseas in Africa by focusing on genealogies of relations between Italy and Libya. She has shown how external borders become a set of complex multidimensional entities. The concept of borderscapes helped her to highlight the role of competing and contradictory temporalities and 'border variations' in different periods.

In addition to Africa, the EU has been transposing its borders throughout the European continent as well. One of those inside-Europe borderscapes has been formed within the territory of so-called Western Balkans. The role of the WB as one of the EU borderscapes is to protect the EU core countries from unwanted migrants. It is produced as a complex transnational, processual, deterritorialized and dispossessed (Brambilla 2015, 221) space. In order to explain how the WB has been constructed as the external borderscape of the EU, we will describe historical and socio-political genealogies of the WB, including the position of Serbia within these processes. Special emphasis will be put on the regulative mechanisms of citizenship regimes – and in particular the EU Accession process, which figures as the main frame of the (external) borderscape production.

The term Balkan itself is contested: Todorova argues that the Balkan has been seen as 'anti-civilisation, alter-ego, the dark side within' Europe (Todorova 2009, 188). This half-imaginary half-real space of the Western Balkans has been conceptualized, from the outside, as inner outskirt of the EU: the shady area outside the Schengen zone and European Union. It is the place whose nationals seek asylum in the EU in vain (the recognition rate for nationals of the WB states is the lowest and they still comprise a significant proportion of asylum seekers in the EU member states) (European Migration Network 2018; European Commission 2018) and an incubator of work-force for deficitary professions in the EU (European Western Balkans 2018). In search for lower costs of production, especially lower wages, European industries are being exported to WB states (Clean Clothes Campaign 2017). WB states have been characterized as having 'fragile economies', high unemployment rate (World Bank Group 2017), corruption, weak institutions, questionable rule of law (GRECO 2018), and diminishing political rights and civil liberties (Freedom House 2019). Austerity measures imposed by the International Monetary Fund following the commonly named 2008 financial crisis, forbade additional employment in the public sector without the approval of special governmental commissions, and led to further deterioration of the already extremely vulnerable sector of civil services. Due to the persistent economic and political problems, WB states are mostly states of emigration (European Council on Foreign Relations 2018).

The European Union executes what is designated as a regional approach in regard to the WB states, which began as a conflict management strategy (Žarin 2007, 518) following hostilities embedded in nationalist paradigms that unfolded throughout 1990s and extends to present times. After the Thessaloniki summit in 2003, this regional approach firmly included the alleged European future for the Western Balkans states, that is, the prospect to finally become members of the EU, the concrete realization of which would be financially, and in other ways, supported by the EU. As a consequence, states had to maintain good mutual relations, build statehoods based on 'the rule of law' and, after positive evaluation by the EU, begin with the implementation of concrete legislative and institutional changes within their territories. Among the first goals was to remove these states from the so-called black Schengen list, that is, to abolish the visa regime for the citizens of the WB states. In order to achieve that, states had to adopt migration policies complementary to those existing in the EU. That implied introducing the asylum system based on the Geneva Convention and 'illegal migration combat strategies' with corresponding institutions, concepts, technologies and practices, which did not exist before this, at least not in the same form (see Kačarska 2012; Đorđević 2013; Stojić Mitrović 2014). The baseline of these changes was to impose control of the movement of WB and third states nationals towards the EU member states, for which the states received financial and other support from the EU directly and through the NGO sector.

Except for Croatia from 2013, WB states are not members of the European Union but are in different stages of the EU accession process, which demands that the non-EU states involved transform their legislative and institutional arrangements in line with the EU administration. This also implies that these states have been, to various degrees, integrating into the EU administrative system for migration control, cooperating with European institutions for migration management, as well as accessing European funds dedicated to these matters. However, the differences between the WB states are becoming muted over time as they become part of the expansive European border regime.

Similarly, all are in a subordinate relation to the EU, with very limited possibilities to negotiate the terms of the accession. The asymmetric political and economic positioning between WB states and the EU is prevailing. This asymmetry is, for instance, exemplified in the negotiations between European Border and Coast Guard Agency (Frontex) with Serbia (and Northern Macedonia) where the EU proposed that 'members of the (Frontex) team shall enjoy immunity' from the administrative, civil and criminal jurisdiction of the Republic of Serbia (Statewatch 2017).

The structural similarities among the WB states outweigh any differences, which mostly concern temporal aspect of the negotiation process (how many chapters a state managed to open, how many agreements to sign) and more local neuralgic issues (relationship between Serbia and Kosovo, issue of the entities in Bosnia and Herzegovina, question of Albanian speaking citizens of Northern Macedonia, etc.) as well as changing physical features of the migration movements.

Serbia began to implement EU-centred migration policy as part of the change of political course following the 2000 overthrow of Slobodan Milosevic's regime. Before this, Serbia (and Yugoslavia) did recognize asylum and refugee status, but in a specific manner; they were both closely related to protection from political persecution and therefore in practice granted to political allies. The 1990s wars of Yugoslav succession brought hundreds of thousands of people from other Yugoslav republics to Serbia, and the word refugee became associated with this particular migration (Stojić Mitrović 2014). On the other hand, Serbia (and Yugoslavia) did not recognize the specific migration type that is now often framed as 'irregular migration' in the politically saturated discourse, whether in its securitarian or humanitarian form. Until the start of the EU accession process, Serbian authorities knew about the offence of illegal border crossing but did not have a specific administrative rubric that would apply to a whole category of people with very specific and often highly derogatory connotations attached to it.

At the external borders of the EU, the only citizenship that counts is the citizenship of the EU member-states. External borderscapes are institutionalized to prevent unwanted migrants from reaching this goal. The asylum system in Serbia, as part of its citizenship regime, is one of the ways borders have been enforced in particular ways to regulate border crossing and access to the EU.

The discourse concerning asylum and irregular migration, with all its concepts and institutions, techniques and code of conduct, was introduced in Serbia through the EU Accession process. As a prerequisite for visa liberalization with the EU (2009), Serbia signed readmission agreements with the EU and its member-states and adopted the Law on Asylum (2007) and the Alien Law (2008). In several national documents, such as, for example, Strategy for Integrated Border Management 2006, or Strategy for Combating Illegal Migration 2009–2014, control of migration toward the EU has explicitly been stated. Citizens of Serbia were promised facilitated access into 'the Area of Freedom, Security and Justice' (Consolidated Version of the Treaty of the Functioning of European Union 2008) only if the strict control over the crossing of Serbian borders was established, and if the Serbian state obliged itself to readmit all its citizens staying without permissions in the EU, as well as third countries nationals who are not allowed to enter and stay in the EU. Facilitating entry into the EU for some is contingent on preventing others from moving freely, and readmission obligations for those who manage to cross despite all. In that way, the EU transferred the control of crossing its external borders to the institutions of a state which itself is not an EU member-state, while the EU kept its supervisory role in this process. Moreover, to enable this enterprise running smoothly, the EU provided necessary aid in trainings, human resources, finances and technical means. Conceptually, administratively and function-ally, the EU Accession process established Serbia as a buffer zone.

Until 'the summer of migration', Serbia's position within the external borderscape was still largely perceived as concerning its own nationals, whose movement it had to control and whose migration to the EU it had to prevent. In the summer 2015, different people came in the focus of the restrictive migration policy: those escaping wars and poverty from the countries south and east of Europe.

From transit to circularity: the vicious circle of the Western Balkans borderscape

The external borderscape is not a stabilized space but a dynamic one constantly in flux. It has been defined and redefined in the historical processes of social institutionalization. As Brambilla has shown, 'border variations' emerge in different periods (Brambilla 2014, 222). In this section, by taking Serbia as an example, we will show how the WB external borderscape has changed between 2008 and 2018 and been reconceptualized from a transit space to a space of circular movement.

Even though Serbia established its asylum system in 2008, it has never become fully operational. The Asylum Office (Kancelarija za azil) has granted refugee status to 55 people and subsidiary protection to 74 from the time of its establishment till 31 December 2018 (BCHR 2019a). Besides the proverbial malfunctioning of the relevant national institutions, the majority of asylum procedures have been suspended, because the applicants simply left the territory of Serbia (BCHR 2019b). The length of stay in Serbia varies drastically, depending on the period of year, current state of the permeability of borders, as well as the individual health and financial situations of migrants. The stay is always the consequence of inability to continue the journey towards the intended destination state.

Since Serbia officially became a part of the European border regime in 2008, the physical features of the migration movements regarding above all the routes, lengths of stay and availability of state-provided accommodation have changed drastically (Beznec, Speer and Stojić Mitrović 2016). Previously, the main migration routes went from the south (Northern Macedonia) and south-east (Bulgaria) to the north (Hungary). These two routes intersected in Serbia's capital, Belgrade. When the Hungarian border became closed in September 2015, the route diverted westward to Croatia. From then until March 2016, the formalized corridor enabled fast, and often state-supported transportation from the border between Greece and Northern Macedonia, across Serbia, Croatia and Slovenia to Austria (Beznec et al., 2016). Its closure, accompanied with the implementation of highly repressive and violent border control practices in Hungary and Croatia, an increase of chain push-backs from the EU states and overall reinforcement of restrictive migration policies resulted in the intensifying of the so-called secondary movements within the region of the Western Balkans.

In Serbia, the differences between entrance and exit borders are erased, since all borders are being crossed in all directions in the attempt to avoid being stuck and to keep alive the hope of reaching final destinations. During a cricket game in an improvised settlement in Horgos in May 2018, a young man said: 'I came here a week ago from Obrenovac (official camp). I came with my friend. He left for Bosnia now. He will tell me what is the situation there. If it is better than here, I will go there.' As the analysis of various NGOs reports shows, sometimes the number of people who entered a state as a result of a collective expulsion is higher than the number of newly arriving people (UNHCR 2018a). It is not uncommon to see people who had never been in Serbia pushed to Serbia from Croatia or Hungary.[3] Some people have also chosen to go back to Greece to try getting to Italy by sea (see also UNHCR 2018b).[4] Some people are arriving for a second time to Serbia: they had already passed but got deported back and are now trying again.[5] As a result of closed borders, the number of cross-border migration movements is doubling. There has also been an extreme proliferation of routes throughout the region. Frontex's annual risk report for the Western Balkans states: 'Specifically, stranded migrants were likely detected several times while attempting to leave the region or at several different border sections, maintaining pressure on certain borders despite the decrease in the actual size of the transiting flow' (Frontex 2018, 21). The European border regime is thus increasing cross-border mobility and producing new forms of despair and vulnerabilities, but also jobs in securitarian and humanitarian industries in its wide borderscapes, where complex, dynamic and amorphous spatialities and social relations are being materialized and negotiated in contested bordering and debordering practices (compare Mezzadra and Neilson 2013).

The social, political, and economic productivity of the European border regime is exemplified in the proliferation of the actors involved in migration processes. The crisis and emergency discourse enabled the imposition of extraordinary measures, accumulation of finances, and allocation of other resources (Stojic Mitrovic 2018). In impoverished WB states, the intake of money from the EU migration emergency and post-emergency funds provided a source of income and thus some sort of economic stability for many people employed in both humanitarian and border control domain. In Serbia, the ban on employment in the state sector was bypassed by channelling the employment and the salaries through the non-governmental organizations, which were employing workers to work for the state institutions.[6] The non-governmental sector increased activities through various programs related to migration, from humanitarian to educational, and local people benefited from trade of goods and services, improved roads and social services (for example, in some villages the schools have been renovated, while in others ambulances have been established, etc.) (Stojić Mitrović and Đurić Milovanović 2019). Furthermore, Serbia benefited from the emergency frame politically, as, to paraphrase the chief of the Working Group for Solving the Problem of Mixed Migration Flows, it built the image of the state which 'can manage the crisis and respect human rights of migrants while doing so' (Radio Television of Vojvodina 2016).

Circular transit is, therefore, the dominant form of migration movements in the region as people look for a way out. However, migrants are not the only ones circulating in the WB: practices, discourses, knowledges, technologies, even particular narratives, organizations and individual-professionals are also following the changed topography. Frontex, for example, is signing new cooperation agreements with WB states (The Delegation of the European Union to the Republic of Serbia 2017); border guards from different states have trainings together to learn from each other and to bring new equipment and manpower to the existing units (Austrian Presidency of the Council of the European Union 2018). Together with people, securitarian practices are circulating, ranging from learning how to directly prevent movement to developing and implementing various deterrence techniques. The circulation of the humanitarian regime organizations is not a new phenomenon; even before the inclusion of WB states into the European border regime were its concepts and practices introduced to (future) practitioners through various trainings.[7] The emergency paradigm brought new organizations, whose regional coordinators followed the humanitarian emergencies across borders, transferring the same more or less failed or successful 'best practices' (how to work with migrants, how to organize their accommodation, what aid to bring and when, and how to 'deal' with the local communities).[8] Small charity NGOs and individual volunteers are also moving across the WB borderscape, together with migrants.[9] Activists are connecting into international solidarity networks. The same narratives are being spread through the region as well, from the initial 'we have empathy for the people who are forced to flee, because we had similar experience in the recent past' (Peović Vuković 2017, 174) to the already annoyed 'migrants are disrupting the way of life in our community', and 'migrants bring crime and diseases' (Peović Vuković 2017, 176–180).

Forced mobility inside the borderscape goes hand in hand with discourses that identify WB states as transit states, giving legitimacy to approaches that treat migration as a transient, emergency-like phenomenon, and instead of building a system that would enable any kind of long-term and substantial integration of migrants into local societies. Many accounts stress the flaws of the asylum system, which functions as the only way to legalize stay, difficulties to access job market, learn language, go to school, and rent a flat, etc. (BCHR 2019b). People are often left without support for many needs beyond emergency reception (food, roof, acute injuries).

Further, the closure of the corridor and the so-called EU–Turkey deal is presented as the 'solution for the crisis', leading to the perception that Europe is in a post-emergency phase. This assumes that the states re-gained control over migration movements and that humanitarian reception should be replaced by projects focusing on integration into the existing state system (primarily education and labour market) (Stojic Mitrovic 2018). This curtailed the access to the emergency funds, resulting in stricter control of finances and re-establishment of the states, and not the civil sector organizations, as the main partners for the implementation of the EU programs.[10]

Migrants' housingscapes

In this context of borderscapes, where bordering processes are affirmed and contested, produced and disrupted, and where different actors clash in asserting dominance over interpretations, concepts, and practices, accommodation of migrants represents one of the main *loci* of disagreement and negotiations. The places of accommodation, of increased migrants' presence, thus become available for political use, which is differently actualized in different circumstances by different actors and for different audiences. Following Brambilla, who uses the notion of 'scapes', and in particular oasis-scape, camp-scape and business-scape, to structure her analyses of complex relations within European external borderscape in Africa (Brambilla 2015), in this text, we introduce a new 'scape' that enables us to conceptualize a focal point where discourses, practices and places that constitute border on the periphery of Europe come together: migrant housingscapes. Brambilla has developed a borderscapes approach in connection to multiple scapes that have been theorized by Appadurai (1996) – including ethnoscapes, technoscapes, financescapes, mediascapes, ideoscapes – in order to introduce processual understanding of contemporary borders as institutions that function in dialectical relation with migration as a social force (Brambilla 2015, 221). We will use the concept of housingscapes in order to speak about paradoxes, contradictions, leakages, instabilities of contemporary bordering emplacements and their particular spatial/temporal variations.

Migrant housingscapes are produced in spaces of the intersection of different housing options including state-run camps and self-organized migrant squats. They are produced topographically, with certain physical features, and topologically, through relations and interplay of different actors and elements. Official institutionalization of 'bordering through housing' has been materialized topographically in different types of camps. The official accommodation of migrants in Serbia can be divided into two large categories, depending on the actor that is organizing accommodation: the state and/or the municipality, or the private sector. State institutions, in particular the Commissariat for Refugees and Migrations of the Republic of Serbia (CRMRS, Komesarijat za izbeglice i migracije Republike Srbije), the Ministry of Labour, Employment, Veteran and Social Policy of the Republic of Serbia (Ministarstvo za rad, zapošljavanje, boračka i socijalna pitanja), and, rarely, municipalities are responsible for three types of open facilities – asylum centres, transit centres and reception centres, while the Ministry of the Interior of the Republic of Serbia (Ministarstvo unutrašnjih poslova Republike Srbije) runs closed facilities, such as jails or Shelter for Foreigners (Prihvatilište za strance). Emergency accommodation has also been occasionally organized by CRMRS and/or municipalities and mosques. The accommodation of certain vulnerable categories (newly arrived families or unaccompanied minors) is carried out in three shelters run by NGOs. Migrants cannot legally rent a place to stay by themselves, but the accommodation has been rented for them by other individuals, charities or NGOs. They can also find or build an improvised shelter individually or collectively.

The state-run camps of the open type have been, over time, opening, closing, and changing which populations they accept. Asylum centres, for the accommodation of persons who showed the intention to seek asylum, were the dominant form of camps until 2015, when the emergency paradigm accompanied with the pressure to somehow impose control over the arrival of people, pushed the state toward opening One Stop Centre camps on the entry points, which were intended only for registration and, to a much lesser extent – distribution of the most urgent aid. Similarly, on the exit points, the state organized transit centres, where people waited for transportation to the border with Hungary or Croatia. The maximum waiting/accommodation time was less than 72 h. Camps were thus officially used to enable the acceleration of transit movement. The capacities (number of beds, winterization and socializing or education areas) of the transit and registration centres were improved after the closure of the corridor, and new reception centres were opened throughout the country in order to fulfil the Serbian offer to assist the EU by taking in up to 6000 persons (Novosti 2015).

Camps have been recognized as spaces that confine migrants and produce them into non-citizens in waiting (Isin and Rygiel 2007, 184; etc.). In recent writings of some authors, camps have further been theorized as lived spaces (Rygiel 2011) where the ordinary and exceptional merge (Giaccaria and Minca 2011). It is precisely these features that open up the space of camp beyond its own borders into the 'scape'. Moreover, as migrant housingscapes are liable to different interpretations and uses, practically and politically they can serve to contain and disrupt the movement of people, but also to enable mobility.

As concerns the topological aspect of housingscaping in Serbia, the state officially fully controls the entrance and exit of people into the camps, migrants and others alike. For example, organizations of the civil sector, NGO workers, journalists, activists and researchers cannot enter the camps without permission from the authorities. This means that aid programs cannot reach migrants without knowledge and approval of the state authorities. Each camp is regulated by house rules, which differ from camp to camp. Similarly, conditions in the camps can vary drastically. Administrators of the camps decide on house rules as well as on which organizations are permitted to enter. This imposes a set of problems to the NGO sector. Not only that the possibility of being disabled from reaching their beneficiaries in the camps, which could lead to the loss of funding, but the civil sector also faces another dilemma: 'We cannot criticize how the centre is being run because we could be denied entrance and then we could not do our job anymore. We cannot speak about the violence in the camp, because we will be pushed out and then no one would be there to protect people during the night.'[11] This situation influences which information emerges from the camps and allows the state institutions to build a certain image while silencing potentially critical voices.

However, in everyday practices, control of the movement of migrants through the camps and access to its services is much less regularized than the control over the entrance and exit of non-state actors. 'You need special permission from Hungarian authorities to approach no-man's land. We (CRMRS) also need special permissions, you see (showing his identification card on the chest). It is a hell of a procedure. If our name is not on the list with border police, we cannot enter. Only they (migrants) can come and go as they wish. But they use that path (pointing to dirt road beside the border fence), not legal entry (pointing to Serbian border police container).'[12]

In terms of laws, the right to use state-managed facilities is given to all persons who have expressed the intention to seek asylum in Serbia. And yet, people who did not apply for asylum, and have no intentions of doing so, are also accommodated in official camps. This is not regulated either by the Alien or Asylum law but interpreted as a kind of emergency response. As a result, official facilities for the accommodation of migrants are in legal limbo and migrants are put in an extra-legal, tolerated status. The fact that the laws concerning migration movements in Serbia are 'open for interpretation' follows its migration management attempts from the start: until the increase of capacities after the closure of the corridor, the number of available beds had often been insufficient for all the people who wanted accommodation in state-run camps. Collective self-organized migrant housing has been taking the form of 'jungles,' located, like state-run camps, in close proximity to the main routes and crossroads, and near the borders with Hungary and Croatia, with tents and makeshift houses on vacant land, or the form of squatted abandoned and damaged structures, including ex-industrial facilities and farm buildings and houses.

In practice, self-organized migrant settlements have often been established not only at the physical edges of the state-run camps, leaning on their fences, but also inside their yards (Ombudsman 2013). 'He (the administrator of the camp in Bogovadja) threatens that he would kick out from the camp anyone (of the official tenants) who gives us a blanket', said a man belonging to one of the 20 persons squatting in the yard of the camp in April 2015, and added, 'But he allows us to be here, and have a fire'. The communication and movement of occupants between the two major types of accommodation, state-run and self-organized, has been possible to various extents depending on the concrete camp and period. Not only were the occupants of squats often able to access electricity or water in the official camps, openly, or under the radar of the camp administrations, but also the occupants of state-run camps were able to access the services of NGOs nominally intended for those who stayed out of the direct state provision, such as medical aid, cooked meals or showers. 'I come to MSF because for the doctor in the camp you must wait. I can't wait; I have a problem. I must see the doctor now,' said a man from Krnjaca camp in October 2017. Moreover, occupants of state-run camps are commonly socializing in squats.[13]

As staying in Serbia is not the desired option, but a consequence of inability to go further, camps are used as temporary resting infrastructure, a place where people meet, make contacts and receive useful information regarding the situation in 'the game'.[14] In other words, camps are used to facilitate movement and not only to contain it. Even some services provided to migrants go hand in hand with this imagery: 'The German language course is a genuine hit! The groups are full, they regularly come and they are totally prepared for classes,' commented an NGO worker in Belgrade in November 2016. 'We have arranged that when they finish the course in sewing, they receive a certificate which they can show to their employer in Germany,' a worker from another NGO said in September 2017.

Brambilla (2015, 400) has argued that we should see borderscape as a common good, a step in which to build a different geopolitical imagination. She also argues that this is possible only if we maintain antagonistic relationship towards state and capital. Migrants and their allies have been using the housing infrastructure in the external borderscapes to produce debordering circulation despite and against forced circulation imposed by Serbia and the EU. They have been utilizing it in order to survive, circulate knowledge and information, technologies, service exchange, solidarity networks, and mutual care. While describing the atmosphere in one of the self-organized camps in the border zone, a young man noticed that temporary housing facilities were the place where one could get life-saving information in the quickest way. These acts of migration, as Papadopoulos and Tsianos describe them, make 'the world of mobile commons'. This world circulates knowledge and practices that people generate, as a continuation of their everyday life (Linebaugh, 2008 in: Papadopoulos and Tsianos 2013) in order to facilitate freedom of movement (Papadopoulos and Tsianos 2013).

Besides cross-border movement, inside the WB borderscape, movement is accelerated within national borders not only in search of exit routes but also as a consequence of economic dependence of Serbian migration management on the funds from the EU: the main mode for deciding on funding both for the state and the civil sector is headcount: more migrants, more potential beneficiaries, mean more money. 'People are money', said a CRMRS worker in an interview from May 2016. 'We receive 8 Euro per person per day. If we do not have enough people, we cannot pay for the costs, electricity, rent, salaries.'[15] This is mentioned as one of the reasons people are transferred from one camp to another. 'When a man goes for "the game", we hold his bed for 72 h. If he fails to cross the border, he can come back. If not, his place becomes available for another one.'[16] In addition, self-organized camps have been regularly raided in order to provide camps with a sufficient number of heads. People were forcibly moved from self-organized squats to state-run facilities to provide the needed balance of people. This points to the question of methodologies of counting.

The topology and topography of housingscapes in Serbia was crucially affected by the securitarian turn of the EU migration policy. Until 2016, the state did not prevent activists and civil sector organizations from reaching people in self-organized settlements. The interference of the state in the work of the civil sector culminated in November 2016 with the 'open letter' sent to all humanitarian aid providing organizations. The letter said explicitly that aid distribution outside state-run camps would not be tolerated. In the letter, aid distribution outside state centres was interpreted as a pull factor and a support of the parallel system. This letter did have an effect, in a way;

NGOs stopped adequate and open distribution of aid to migrants and had to resort to secrecy and smaller distribution, choosing the most vulnerable, and leaving migrants abandoned in dire circumstances.

The engine pushing these changes was the end of the emergency phase and the European border regime's securitarian turn. The state wanted to show that it was capable of fulfilling its promise to accommodate a couple of thousand migrants, who, on the contrary, preferred self-organized housing. In order to have the camps running, it had to have a certain number of persons accommodated inside. Therefore, it resorted to various methods to 'attract' people, besides making lives outside state-run camps more difficult. One, which is still covered in a layer of controversy, is the 'waiting lists' for entering Hungary through the 'transit zones' (Lanzarote Committee 2017). Allegedly, in July 2016 Serbia made an agreement with Hungary to allow migrants to apply for asylum from camps in Serbia and wait there for invitations into the transit zones for interviews. Hungarian authorities deny the existence of any agreement that cedes rights to a foreign state to decide who would enter Hungary (Lanzarote Committee 2017, 13). An epidemic of scabies was also used to highlight that adequate treatment could only be conducted inside state-organized facilities and that migrants not only should go into the camps but also that the entrance and exit in and outside the camps should become more restricted (Blic 2016).

In 2016, state officials said that the donors (the EU) should not give money to the nongovernmental sector, because it had not been involved in managing the migration crisis. 'We are not asking for money to be given to those who turned [the migrant crisis] into business. For us, the migrant crisis has not become business. We are asking for money for military and police, for the state organs which are involved in managing migrant centres, border protection, etc.', (Radio Television of Serbia 2016). This attempt of the state to be acknowledged as the main actor of the migration management in Serbia was hindered by a growing number of accounts depicting the hardships migrants were enduring in Serbia in the 2016–2017 winter. This enabled existing NGOs to resume their work while bringing new solidarity forces to Serbia. Groups of international activists began to operate in Serbia, first in the 'Belgrade barracks', and, after their demolition in May 2017, in border areas. Their work in border areas enabled the international public to become aware of push-backs from Hungary and Croatia and the violence to which migrants were regularly exposed by border units.[17] The reports show that the vast majority of those who try to cross the border end up being pushed back to Serbia: 'They are denied access to the asylum procedures, often brutally attacked by EU border authorities and deported back to marginal and temporary living conditions (…)' (No Name Kitchen 2018, 2). These reports rarely receive attention from the mainstream media, adding to the dominance of a particular image of borderscape, preferred by the state and the EU. Some of these groups spread their activities in Bosnia and Herzegovina in 2018, confirming through their practice the prevalence of similar structural features across the WB borderscape.

Conclusion

The concept of borderscape is invaluable for understanding how the externalization of EU border regime functions. It is not only the law and the legal discourses that define the border, but an assemblage of discourses, practices, technologies and spaces. Starting from the neo-colonial construct of the Western Balkans, this paper shows how the EU created one of its buffer zones. Political, social and economic challenges served as a base to legitimize the exceptionalization of the 'infantilized' Balkans into a space that needs EU guidance, making it dependent and accountable to the EU core. The WB are governed by hierarchical structures of power that are deciding on and influencing practices and policies, as well as by the hierarchical structure of citizenships, the effects of which reach all domains of social and political life. These structures are transferred onto borders in order to control their permeability. They are at the foundation of producing the WB borderscapes and their conflicting imaginaries of sovereignty and territoriality, constructed through a constant interplay of bordering, debordering and rebordering processes.

In this article, we focus on the dominant features of the Western Balkan borderscape through the example of Serbia. We demonstrate what the European border regime (with its securitarian turn and official closure of the corridor in 2016) does to the territory of the WB borderscape. Namely, it has transformed it from a zone of unidirectional transit to a zone of (forced) circular movement. Forced circular movement, from camp to camp and across the territories of the WB nation-states, is used to enact a form of mobile detention. Confinement through mobility (Tazzioli 2018) *is de facto* exclusion through mobility. Not only does the right to mobility represent a form of social and political capital, but asymmetric power relations can be manifested also in pushing people into mobility. In this hierarchical conglomerate of territories, sovereignties and political influence, of cores and borderscapes, migrations are on the one hand managed by securitarian practices and humanitarian regimes, and on the other disrupted by autonomous movement of people, activists, and support networks, as well as knowledge, discourses and technologies that are circulating in the external borderscape.

Housing has been serving as one of the major 'scapes' of circulation. In the external borderscape, state-run camps are not the only spatial referent. Together with camps, self-organized migrant squats create a micro-scape of housing. In these conditions, housingscapeing has been a tangible expression of the attempts to de-institutionalize the border. External-border housingscape has been used by migrants to disrupt the enforced circulation and to reproduce and enhance the circulation of a mobile commons, demonstrating profound disobedience toward the dispositif of the border exercised by the more powerful actors.

A borderscape approach (Brambilla 2014, 240) has the potential to make the invisible visible. Serbia has produced a spectacular image of a stabilized external border for the EU. In this way, the movement has been hidden and people on the move silenced. In this article, we have used the borderscape 'method' to reveal the dialectics of what is visible and invisible in the external border and to re-conceptualize the spectacularized space of the EU and national bordering practices.

Notes

1 Albania, Bosnia and Herzegovina, Northern Macedonia, Kosovo, Montenegro and Serbia; Croatia left this group in 2013, when it became an EU member-state.
2 We use the concept of dispositif as an apparatus as well as the image of a cross-section of current relations between institutions, practices, actors, technologies, knowledges and so on (compare Sverre, Gudmand-Høyer, and Thaning 2016).

3 Interview with NGO worker, Belgrade, Serbia, October 2018.

4 Interview with a migrant, Belgrade, Serbia, October 2018.

5 Interview with CRMRS worker, Belgrade, September 2018.

6 Interview with CRMRS worker, Belgrade, Serbia, September 2018.

7 Interview with former IOM trainer for CRMRS, conducted in Belgrade in December 2014. 'We taught them that they could not use the phrase "illegal migrant" in official documents, but "irregular migrant" instead, because of all connotations it entails'.

8 Interviews with NGO workers in Belgrade and Subotica, Serbia, in January and May 2018.

9 No Name Kitchen and BelgrAid (now Collective aid), for example, spread activities from Serbia to Bosnia and Herzegovina.

10 Bosnia and Herzegovina, which is discursively framed as facing a 'postponed migration crisis', a kind of collateral damage, or secondary crisis deriving directly from the 'solution' of the primary one, is just at the beginning of this process.

11 Interview with NGO worker, Berkasovo, Serbia, September 2017.

12 Conversation with CRMRS worker, improvised settlement in Tompa-Roszke border-crossing, May 2016.

13 The stated reasons can vary significantly: 'I come to (Belgrade) barracks to meet people, my friends. I got the camp, they did not. We meet here, they can't come to the camp.' (Belgrade, January 2017); 'I come here, because these guys (volunteers from an NGO providing showers) are great. We play cards, smoke. We have fun. Girls are beautiful.' (Sombor, May 2018); 'We cook what we like here.' (Sombor, May 2018) and so on.

14 'The game' is a phrase used by migrants for the often risky and physically dangerous attempts to cross the borders in the 'endles cycle of border-crossing' (MSF 2017, 2).

15 Interview with CRMRS worker, Sandzak area, May 2014.

16 Interview with CRMRS worker, Belgrade, Serbia, May 2018.

17 No Name Kitchen violence reports are available at: https://www.nonamekitchen.org/en/violence-reports/

Acknowledgments

We would like to thank to all the people that we had a chance to meet and talk to and to the collectives No Name Kitchen, Rigardu, Escuela con Alma and Collective aid for their trust. The authors thank to anonymous peer reviewers, and to our dear friends and colleagues Mirjana Morokvašić-Müller, Maple Razsa and Chloe Powers for their feedback and suggestions. The struggle goes on.

Disclosure statement

No potential conflict of interest was reported by the authors.

Funding

This article has been conducted within the framework of the project No. 177027 Multiethnicity, multiculturalism, migrations – contemporary processes of the Institute of Ethnography of the Serbian Academy of Sciences and Arts, funded by the Ministry of Education, Science, and Technological Development of the Republic of Serbia as well as by European Comision's Horizon 2020 research and innovation programme under the Marie Sklodowska-Curie grant for the research project HOUSEREG, agreement No. 707848.

References

Appadurai, A. 1996. *Modernity at Large: Cultural Dimensions of Globalization.* Minneapolis: University of Minnesota Press.

Beznec, B., M. Speer, and M. Stojić Mitrović. 2016. *Governing the Balkan Route: Macedonia, Serbia, and the European Border Regime.* Belgrade: Rosa Luxemburg Stiftung for Southeast Europe.

Boccagni, P., and A. M. Brighenti. 2017. "Immigrants and Home in the Making: Thresholds of Domesticity, Commonality and Publicness." *Journal of Housing and the Built Environment* 32 (1): 1–11. doi:10.1007/s10901-015-9487-9.

Brambilla, C. 2014. "Shifting Italy/Libya Borderscapes at the Interface of EU/Africa Borderland: A "Genealogical" Outlook from the Colonial Era to Post-Colonial Scenarios." *ACME: an International E Journal for Critical Geographies* 13 (2): 220–245.

Brambilla, C. 2015. "From Border as a Method of Capital to Borderscape as a Method for a Geographical Opposition to Capitalism." In *Bollettino Della Società Geografica Italiana Roma - Series XIII, Vol. VIII, Issue 3*, edited by A. Turco, 393–402.

Collinson, S. 1996. "Visa Requirements, Carrier Sanctions, 'Safe Third Countries' and 'Readmission': The Development of an Asylum 'Buffer Zone' in Europe." *Transactions of the Institute of British Geographers* 21 (1): 76–90.

De Genova, N., and M. Tazzioli. 2016. "Europe / Crisis: Introducing New Keywords of "The Crisis" in and of 'Europe." In *Europe/Crisis: New Keywords of 'The Crisis' in and of 'Europe'*, edited by N. De Genova and M. Tazzioli, 2–7. Near Futures Online 1: "Europe at Crossroads". http://nearfuturesonline.org/europecrisis-new-keywords-of-crisis-in-and-of-europe/

Đorđević, B. 2013. "Politics of Return, Inequality and Citizenship in the Post-Yugoslav Space." *CITSEE Working Paper Series 2013/29.* Edinburg: University of Edinburg.

Giaccaria, P., and C. Minca. 2011. "Topographies/Topologies of the Camp: Auschwitz as a Spatial Threshold." *Political Geography* 30 (1): 312. doi:10.1016/j.polgeo.2010.12.001.

Hameršak, M., and I. Pleše. 2017. "Zarobljeni U Kretanju: O Hrvatskoj Dionici Balkanskog Koridora." In *Kamp, Koridor, Granica: Studije Izbjegliištva U Suvremenom Hrvatskom Kontekstu*, edited by E. Bužinkić and M. Hameršak, 9–39. Zagreb: Institut za etnologiju i folkloristiku.

Isin, E., and K. Rygiel. 2007. "Abject Spaces: Frontiers, Zones, Camps." *In the Logics of Biopower and the War on Terror: Living, Dying, Surviving*, edited by E. Dauphinee and C. Masters, 181–203. London: Palgrave Macmillan.

Jagetic Andersen, D., and R. E. Pedersen. 2018. "Practicing Home in the Foreign: The Multiple Homing Practices of Artisan Journeymen on the Tramp." *Nordic Journal of Migration Research* 8 (2): 82–90. doi:10.1515/njmr-2018-0003.

Kačarska, S. 2012. "Europeanisation through Mobility: Visa Liberalisation and Citizenship Regimes in the Western Balkans." *CITSEE Working Paper Series 2012/21.* Edinburg: University of Edinburg. doi:10.1094/PDIS-11-11-0999-PDN.

Kasparek, B., and M. Speer. 2015. "Of Hope. Hungary and the Long Summer of Migration." Bordermonitoring.eu Accessed February 22, 2019 http://bordermonitoring.eu/ungarn/2015/09/of-hope-en/

Lavenex, S. 1999. *Safe Third Countries. Extending the EU Asylum and Immigration Policies to Central and Eastern Europe*. Budapest: CEU Press.

Liudmila., A., and S. H. Baglama. 2018. "Migration, Metaphor and Myth in Media Representations: The Ideological Dichotomy of 'Them' and 'Us'." *SAGE Open* 8 (2): 1–13.

Stojić Mitrović, M. and A. Đurić Milovanović. 2019. "The Humanitarian Engagement of Faith-Based Organizations in Serbia: Balancing between the *Vulnerable Human* and the *(In)Secure (Nation)State*." In *Forced Migration and Human Security in the Eastern Orthodox World*, edited by L. N. Leaustean, London: Routledge (Forthcoming).

Martin, D. 2015. "From Spaces of Exception to 'Campscapes': Palestinian Refugee Camps and Informal Settlements in Beirut." *Political Geography* 44: 918. doi:10.1016/j.polgeo.2014.08.001.

Mezzadra, S., and B. Neilson. 2013. *Border as Method, Or, the Multiplication of Labor*. Durham: Duke University Press.

MSF. 2017. Serbia. Games of Violence. Unaccompanied children and young people repeatedly abused by EU member state member authorities. Doctors Without Borders. Accessed June 20, 2019. https://www.msf.org/sites/msf.org/files/serbia-games-of-violence-3.10.17.pdf

Musliu, V. 2015. "Mapping Narratives on Failed States. The Case of Kosovo." In *States Falling Apart? Secessionist and Autonomy Movements in Europe*, edited by E. M. Belser, A. Fang, N. Massüger, and R. O. Pillai, 369–381. Bern: Stämpfli Verlag.

Papadopoulos, D., and V. S. Tsianos. 2013. "After Citizenship: Autonomy of Migration, Organisational Ontology and Mobile Commons." *Citizenship Studies* 17: 2. doi:10.1080/13621025.2013.780736.

Papadopoulou-Kourkoula, A. 2008. *Transit Migration. The Missing Link between Emigration and Settlement*. London: Palgrave McMilan.

Peović Vuković, K. 2017. "'Refugee Crisis' and the Speech of the Unconscious." In *Kamp, Koridor, Granica: Studije Izbjeglištva U Suvremenom Hrvatskom Kontekstu*, edited by E. Bužinkić and H. Marijana, 169–198. Zagreb: Institut za etnologiju i folkloristiku.

Petrović, D. 2016. *Izbjeglištvo U Suvremenom Svijetu. Od Političkoteorijskih Utemeljenja Do Biopolitičkih Ishoda*. Zagreb: Ljevak.

Rajaram, P. K., and C. Grundy-Warr. 2007. "Introduction." In *Borderscapes: Hidden Geographies and Politics at Territory's Edge*, edited by P. K. Rajaram and C. Grundy-Warr, IX–XXXIX. Minnesota: University of Minnesota Press.

Rygiel, K. 2011. "Bordering Solidarities: Migrant Activism and the Politics of Movement and Camps at Calais." *Citizenship Studies* 15 (1): 1–19. doi:10.1080/13621025.2011.534911.

Statewatch. 2017. "Frontex in the Balkans: Serbian Government Rejects EU's Criminal Immunity Proposals." Accessed. http://statewatch.org/news/2017/jul/eu-frontex-serbia.htm

Stojić Mitrović, M. 2014. "Serbian Migration Policy Concerning Irregular Migration and Asylum in the Context of the EU Integration Process." *Issues in Ethnology and Anthropology* 9 (4): 1105–1120. doi:10.21301/eap.v9i4.15.

Stojic Mitrovic, M. 2018. "The Reception of Migrants in Serbia: Policies, Practices, and Concepts". In *The Challenges of Migration in Southeast Europe: Social workers as Promotors of Human Rights in the times of Rising Anti-migration Sentiment in the Countries of South East Europe*, edited by J. M. Watkins and D. Zaviršek, 17–27. Advance online publication. doi:10.1007/s41134-018-0077-0

Sverre, R., M. Gudmand-Høyer, and M. S. Thaning. 2016. "[2014]. "Foucault's Dispositive: The Perspicacity of Dispositive Analytics in Organizational Research."." *Organization* 23 (2): 272–298. doi:10.1177/1350508414549885.

Tazzioli, M. 2018. "Containment through Mobility: Migrants' Spatial Disobediences and the Reshaping of Control through the Hotspot System." *Journal of Ethnic and Migration Studies* 44: 16. doi:10.1080/1369183X.2017.1401514.

Tazzioli, M., and G. Garelli. 2018. *Containment beyond Detention: The Hotspot System and Disrupted Migration Movements across Europe*. Environment and Planning D: Society and Space. Advance online publication. doi:10.1177/0263775818759335.

Thouez, C. 2000. "Towards a Common European Migration and Asylum Policy?" *New Issues in Refugee Research Working Paper No. 27*, 1–24.

Todorova, M. N. 2009. *Imagining the Balkans*. New York: Oxford University Press.
Žarin, I. 2007. "EU Regional Approach to the Western Balkans – The Human Security Dimension." *Medunarodni Problemi* 59 (4): 513–545. doi:10.2298/MEDJP0704513Z.

Sources

Alien Law. 2008. *Zakon o strancima RS. Službeni glasnik RS br. 97/2008.* http://paragraf.rs/propisi/zakon_o_strancima.html
Asylum Law. 2007. "Zakon O Azilu RS. Službeni Glasnik RS Br. 109/2007." http://www.ombudsman.lls.rs/attachments/Zakon%20o%20azilu.pdf doi:10.1094/PDIS-91-4-0467B.
Austrian Presidency of the Council of the European Union. 2018. "Western Balkans Conference: Signature of Prüm Agreement for Southeast Europe." https://www.eu2018.at/latest-news/news/09-13-Westbalkan-Konferenz–Pr-m-Abkommen-f-r-S-dosteuropa-unterzeichnet-html
BCHR. 2019a. "Asylum Office Statistics in 2018. Belgrade Centre for Human Rights." http://azil.rs/en/asylum-office-statistics-in-2018/
BCHR. 2019b. "Right to Asylum in the Republic of Serbia 2018. Belgrade Centre for Human Rights." http://azil.rs/en/right-to-asylum-in-the-republic-of-serbia-2018/
Blic. 2016. "Vulin: Control at the Borders, the Number of Migrants Who Enter Serbia Is Controlled. [Vulin: Kontrola Na Granicama, Broj Migranata Koji Uđu U Srbiju Se Kontroliše]." Blic, November 3 2016. https://www.blic.rs/vesti/drustvo/vulin-kontrola-na-granicama-broj-migranata-koji-udu-u-srbiju-se-kontrolise/nwq38p6
Clean Clothes Campaign. 2017. "Europe'S Sweatshops. The Results of CCC's Most Recent Researches in Central, East and South East Europe." https://cleanclothes.org/livingwage/europe/europes-sweatshops
Consolidated Version of the Treaty of Functioning of European Union. 2008. "Official Journal of the European Union C 115/47." https://eur-lex.europa.eu/resource.html?uri=cellar:41f89a28-1fc6-4c92-b1c8-03327d1b1ecc.0007.02/DOC_1&format=PDF
Tomlinson, S. 2015. "March of the Migrants Now 'Out of Control' as Croatia Sends Thousands More Towards Overwhelmed Slovenia, Who are Left to Beg the EU for Help Policing Its Borders." Daily Mail, Octobar 20 2015. https://www.dailymail.co.uk/news/article-3280882/Slovenia-accuses-Croatia-sending-thousands-migrants-borders-without-control-police-escort-arrivals-overcrowded-reception-centre.html
European Commission. 2018. *Progress report on the Implementation of the European Agenda on Migration.* https://ec.europa.eu/home-affairs/sites/homeaffairs/files/what-we-do/policies/european-agenda-migration/20180516_progress-report-european-agenda-migration_en.pdf
European Council on Foreign Relations. 2018. "The Way Back: Brain Drain and Prosperity in the Western. Balkans." https://www.ecfr.eu/publications/summary/the_way_back_brain_drain_and_prosperity_in_the_western_balkans
European Migration Network. 2018. *Safe Countries of Origin - EMN Inform.* Brussels: European Migration Network. https://ec.europa.eu/home-affairs/sites/homeaffairs/files/00_inform_safe_country_of_origin_final_en_1.pdf
European Western Balkans. 2018. "Requests for German Working Visas Double in 2018." https://europeanwesternbalkans.com/2018/09/01/requests-german-working-visas-double-2018/
Freedom House. 2019. "Freedom in the World 2018. Serbia Profile." https://freedomhouse.org/report/freedom-world/2018/serbia
Frontex. 2018. "Western Balkans Annual Risk Analysis 2018." https://reliefweb.int/sites/reliefweb.int/files/resources/WB_ARA_2018.pdf
GRECO. 2018. *Fourth evaluation round Corruption prevention in respect of members of parliament, judges and prosecutors. Compliance report Serbia.* https://rm.coe.int/fourth-evaluation-round-corruption-prevention-in-respect-of-members-of/1680792e56

Lanzarote Committee. 2017. *Special report Further to a visit of a delegation of the Lanzarote Committee to transit zones at the Serbian/Hungarian border (July 5-7 2017).* https://rm.coe.int/special-report-further-to-a-visit-undertaken-by-a-delegation-of-the-la/1680784275

No Name Kitchen. 2018. "Border Violence on the Balkan Route." http://www.nonamekitchen.org/wp-content/uploads/2019/01/Finished-Border-Violence-on-the-Balkan-Route.pdf

V.C.S and G.C. 2015. "Serbia Is Ready for 6000 Refugees. [Srbija Je Spremna Za 6.000 Izbeglica]." Novosti. Octobar 31 2015. http://www.novosti.rs/vesti/naslovna/drustvo/aktuelno.290.html:574480-Srbija-je-spremna-za-6000-izbeglica

Ombudsman. 2013. *National Preventive Mechanism: Report on the Visit to the Asylum Centre in Bogovadja on 14^{th}October 2013.* https://npm.lls.rs/attachments/053_AC%20in%20Bogovadja%202014%20Oct%202013.pdf

Radio Television of Serbia. 2016. "Stefanovic: There Have Been No Concrete Solutions at the Summit [Stefanović: Na Samitu Nije Bilo Konkretnih Rešenja]." http://www.rts.rs/page/stories/sr/story/9/politika/2464714/stefanovic-na-samitu-nije-bilo-konkretnih-resenja.html

Radio Television of Vojvodina. 2016. "Vulin about Migrants in Geneva: Serbia Cannot and Must Not Stay Alone [Vulin U Ženevi O Migrantima: Srbija Ne Može I Ne Sme Da Ostane Sama]." Accessed. http://www.rtv.rs/sr_lat/politika/vulin-u-zenevi-o-migrantima-srbija-ne-moze-i-ne-sme-da-ostane-sama_761638.html

KIRS. 2009. "Strategy for Combating Illegal Migration in the Republic of Serbia 2009-2014." *The Official Gazette of the RS No 25/2009.* http://www.kirs.gov.rs/docs/Strategy%20for%20Combating%20Illegal%20Migration%20in%20the%20Republic%20of%20Serbia.pdf

"Migrant Crisis in Europe." *The Boston Globe* 2015. https://www.bostonglobe.com/news/bigpicture/2015/09/03/migrant-crisis-europe/8fjNUeJ5Lvbnqg31nnMSbO/story.html

The Delegation of the European Union to the Republic of Serbia. 2017. "Leggeri: Frontex Liaison Officer Coming to Serbia, Will Be Responsible for Entire Western Balkans." https://europa.rs/leggeri-frontex-liaison-officer-coming-to-serbia-will-be-responsible-for-entire-western-balkans/?lang=en

"Fear, Fatigue and Separation: A Journey with Migrants Willing to Risk Everything." The Guardian. Accessed April 6, 2015. https://www.theguardian.com/global-development/2015/apr/06/fear-fatigue-separation-migrants-western-balkans-west-africans-eu-back-door

UNHCR. 2018a. *Serbia Update. 01-14 October 2018.* https://data2.unhcr.org/en/documents/download/66323

UNHCR. 2018b. *Snapshot Serbia November 2018.* https://data2.unhcr.org/en/documents/download/67186

World Bank Group. 2017. *Western Balkans Regular Economics Report No 12. Job Creation Picks up. Fall 2017.* https://openknowledge.worldbank.org/bitstream/handle/10986/28883/121417-WP-PUBLIC.pdf?sequence=1&isAllowed=y

For 'common struggles of migrants and locals'. Migrant activism and squatting in Athens

Valeria Raimondi

ABSTRACT

This article analysis the socio-political form of the migrant squats, and the socio-spatial interactions they foster and generate. Drawing on empirical research, it focuses on the Athenian context where, since September 2015, political groups belonging to the anti-authoritarian and Left-libertarian movement, occupied some empty buildings to host migrants in transit through the country. From a political perspective, the squats are interpreted here as strategies of struggle to gain access to the space of the city and they also constitute instances of migrant activism and resistance to the European border regime. Moreover, migrant occupations represent practices and sites for contesting citizenship, intended as a category of political status; as such, they exceed the limits of this category and move beyond the boundaries of the nation-state, originating practices of citizenship 'from below', while at the same time they produce subjectivities that choose to 'opt out' of citizenship as a legal status. This article is situated within the contextualisation of space and autonomy. Migrant squats are looked at from the angle of the 'gaze of autonomy', since they are aimed both at contesting citizenship as an exclusionary feature, and at revindicating the activists' (both migrants and non) presence in the space of city.

Introduction

Two years ago, refugees managed to open the borders of Europe.

They took the road and no one could stop them. Freedom of movement and the right to a life of safety, fundamental rights, and dignity, were no longer just a slogan (City Plaza flyer for 'Welcome United' action, 2–16 September 2017).

In 2015, with the exacerbation of the 'refugee crisis' and the 'long summer of migration' a powerful solidarity movement has taken hold throughout Europe. In Greece, as in other European countries, citizens and social movements mobilised alongside migrants in their everyday struggles for rights and freedom of movement, fighting against exclusion and racism. Solidarity movements found different ways to support migrants: from practical and logistical help in the border areas – in crossing the borders and carrying out sea rescue operations – to the organisation of solidarity camps (i.e. the 'No Border camp' in Thessaloniki in July 2016). The struggles continue beyond the moment of border crossings and the disruptive power of migrants embraces different spatialities and temporalities at narrower scales. In the urban contexts, the experiences of solidarity take different forms, such as physical and political support for migrants in transit – i.e. Athens (Kotronaki 2018; Lafazani 2018; Raimondi 2019) and Rome (Grazioli 2017), or with more long-term practices in cities where they decide to settle – i.e Brussels (Depraetere and Oosterlynck 2017) and Amsterdam (Dadusc, this issue). In most cases, the response from institutions at every level consisted in the repression and criminalisation of such experiences (Dadusc and Mudu 2019). Despite the constant attempts at repression, solidarity has continued in various forms involving heterogeneous groups of people.

In Greece, the solidarity activities were initially concentrated on the landing islands of Lesbos and Chios, the ports of Piraeus and Thessaloniki and the border crossing at Idomeni. Since the Summer of 2015 the political environment changed and the solidarity movements adapted to the new geographical focal points, the major cities in the mainland (Oikonomakis 2018, 66). In this article I focus on the Athenian context where, since September 2015, political groups belonging to the anti-authoritarian and Left-libertarian movement, occupied empty buildings in the city centre to host migrants and refugees in transit through the country.

This article analyses migrant squats as socio-political formations. The implementation of the analysis happens at different spatial scales – from the intimate scale of the individual experience to the wider one of the city. Theoretically, the article develops along the lines of three concepts: citizenship, space and autonomy. Migrant squats are interpreted here as practices and sites for contesting citizenship, intended as a category of political status; as such, they exceed the limits of this category and move beyond the boundaries of the nation-state, originating practices of citizenship 'from below' (Nyers and Rygiel 2012), while at the same time they produce subjectivities that choose to 'opt out' of citizenship as legal status (McNevin 2012). Migrant squats are here ideally put at the intersection of citizenship and space, and looked at from the angle of the 'gaze of autonomy' (Mezzadra 2011), since they are aimed both at contesting citizenship as an exclusionary feature, and at revindicating the activists' (both migrants and non) presence in the space of city. The urban space is central to the dynamics investigated as contemporary urban space is socially produced and transformed by the dynamics triggered by transnational migrations (De Genova 2015, 4) and since cities constitute critical sites for the policing of dissent (Darling 2017b).

This work aims at shedding light on the occupations of migrants and activists as egalitarian political spaces, alternative and in opposition to the institutional reception system and the related legal structure. Migrant squats as autonomous practices of solidarity materialise in the 'intervals of political subjectification' (Rancière 1999, 137) and constitute creative acts, not (only) in the sense of a tangible production, but for the formation of the new subjectivities they render possible (Rancière 2010, 59). In doing so, these laboratories of autonomous reception can be interpreted as an alternative form of enacting citizenship (Mezzadra 2011), and as such they actualise their disruptive potential in the constitution of new political subjects (Squire 2016, 14–15). This formation, however, does not happen without contradictions and the new hybrid subjectivities are characterised by an ambiguous nature that pushes the occupations to a constant reconsideration of their internal dynamics. In other words, when applied to the specific empirical context, the theory should be problematised in relation to the complications that arise from everyday practice.

This paper is based on fieldwork that I undertook in Athens, from November 2016 until September 2017, and from May to September 2018. The data for this article were obtained through qualitative processes, mainly coming through self-ethnography and the practice of militant research (Garelli and Tazzioli 2013). Along with direct observation, semi-structured interviews were held to some of the participants, both anarchists and migrants, although conversations could not always be recorded.

The analysis of political statements of the occupations and anarchist groups, together with the collection of political flyers, allowed a better understanding of the role of the different groups and their specific positions. Furthermore, the participation in assemblies and demonstrations allowed to deepen the knowledge of the political context. The information obtained in situations where it was not possible to define my positionality and clarify my role does not appear in this article for ethical reasons. However, they remain in the background, to build a more complete framework for analysis. In all contexts, priority was given to protecting vulnerable individuals, guaranteeing anonymity and omitting information that could put them in danger.

During my fieldwork I lived in City Plaza Refugee Accommodation and Solidarity Space participating in its activities, as well as being actively involved in the political and social life of Exarcheia. My involvement in City Plaza has allowed me to have an insider point of view on these practices and at the same time to acquire specific knowledge about their internal and external dynamics – between the different social groups that inhabit the squats and with regards to their relations with other political spaces in the city.

A brief explanation is needed in this regard. Although the migrant occupations in Athens have similar characteristics – concerning internal organisation and political stances – at the same time they present substantial differences, due to the very nature of these experiences, and the subjects that compose them. In this article I rely on the common characteristics between the different spaces that I have identified during my experience in the field, but always considering their fundamental differences. For instance, City Plaza itself is difficult to investigate in relation to other practices of squatting, since it represents a quite peculiar experience in the Athenian scenario. Occupied in April 2016, the former hotel has hosted more than two thousand people in transit in the last three years, and it is the largest squat in the city. Even though it takes part in the Coordination of Refugees Squats assembly, the activists who occupied it do not define Plaza as a squat but as a space of self-managed reception. This is related to the fact that their political background is different from the one of the activists from other occupations: former members of Syriza party (a Left-wing party in office in Greece since 2015) they do not refer to themselves as anarchists. This different political affiliation has created distances and tensions between City Plaza and other squats, further enriching the levels of this analysis.

Spaces of citizenship

We create spaces where all the voices which are being silenced can be heard. Spaces open to all those who care about our shared life and coexistence in solidarity. Open to all those who cannot accept that refugees are being subjected to wretched conditions [...] To those who, under harsh conditions, are emigrating and struggle for their lives and futures for years (City Plaza Refugee and Accommodation Space, flyer September 2017).

'Citizenship is about *being there*, legitimately, in public space, and *being seen* to be there'. (McNevin 2012, 167; original emphasis). Space is not a neutral actor, but is called into play in different ways – i.e. to the extent that it is claimed, occupied, transformed, used, produced and represented (Lefebvre 1974). The access to a space is conquered, and this conquest often involves a collective action and a political claim (Harvey 2012). Migrant squats aim to claim a presence in the place where they are enacted. The physical location of the squats – in the heart of the city – is a crucial aspect of their strategy. In fact, by *being there* migrants put in place an embodied taking-up of the public space of the city (McNevin 2012, 177) against the policies that label them as 'outsiders'. In doing so they contest the process of illegalisation and openly declare the legitimacy of their presence, while their presence itself inside the very centre of the city functions as an ongoing reminder of their existence in the everyday life of citizens, 'making what was unseen visible, in getting what was only audible as noise to be heard as speech' (Rancière 2010, 38).

This article aligns with an understanding of citizenship framed through the focus of migrant agency. In examining the experiences of migrant squatting, I draw on Isin's definition of acts of citizenship as 'those acts that transform forms [...] and modes [...] of being political by bringing into being new actors as activist citizens (that is, claimants of rights) through creating or transforming sites and stretching scales' (Isin 2009, 383). In the squats migrants are 'engaged in acts which disrupt citizenship norms yet which are not in themselves aimed at gaining legal or conventional citizen-status' (McNevin 2012, 179). In the contingency of the Greek context, in fact, obtaining a legal status might not be the first aim of migrants – or their 'preferred way', to say it with Hindess (2004) – since living in the squats surely is a way for some undocumented people to remain 'de-identified'[1] (Papadopoulos and Tsianos 2007, 166).

As 'citizenship is [...] inextricably and irreducibly *spatial*, and strongly linked to the material and discursive dimensions of different geographical places and scales' (Maestri and Hughes 2017, 626; original emphasis), the enactment of citizenship 'from below' happens through the creation of 'new *spaces* of citizenship that potentially enable both new ways of being political and new visions for the type of politics we wish to imagine the world' (Nyers and Rygiel 2012, 9; my emphasis). Drawing on Squire's (2016) interpretation of acts as disruptive practices recognisable by the production of new political subjects, the new ways of being political entails the emerging of the new subjectivity of the non-citizen migrant activist. This formation is not a peaceful gesture, but a violent one since it implies the rupture of a scheme, the direct confrontation with the stereotyped image of the 'dangerous migrant' or the 'migrant in need' that characterised the predominantly perceived imaginary of the people in motion.

The disruptive power of migrant occupations and the subversive socialities they render possible become more evident when the space of the squat is interpreted in relation to its institutional counterpart – the refugee camp, spatially idealised as a 'distant and legitimate "other" of the city' (Darling 2017a, 182). Rancière's differentiation between police and politics (Rancière 1995) – between the logics of identification and proper placement, and the opposite logics of disidentification and 'improper' placement – helps framing the experiences of the migrant squats in their (political) antagonism to the nation-state and EU policies. The identification of migrants as 'non-citizens' in order to confine them in the ad-hoc created spaces of the camps (the *police* order) is challenged by the counter-logics of migrants' struggles, crystallised in the squats. In other words, the dominant ordered space of the camp is disrupted by the squat, characterised by commoning practices of sharing and solidarity (Stavrides 2016).

The refugee camp legitimates and materialises the political stances of the European border regime, producing within it the social and spatial hierarchies of the state centric order that underlies the conception of the regime itself. In the vision of this system, the interests, expectations and living conditions of migrant people are relegated to the margins, while those of the reception countries are at the centre. In camps and hotspots[2] migrants become abstract beings, socially and politically subaltern subjects (Avallone 2018, 30), anonymous *bodies* object of the migratory discourse.

Opposed to this vision, migrant squats contribute in building a different view on migration (Sayad 1999). The place of the squat is considered as 'antithetical' to the one of the camp (Raimondi 2019), as migrant squats try to avoid the reproduction of relations of domination and subordination typical of the dispositifs of immigration control where relations of dependency and power are produced and reinforced (Anderson, Sharma, and Wright 2012). Moreover, located in the city centre, the squats counter the alienation and seclusion of the camps, where refugees and asylum seekers are confined in peripheral areas, denying them the right to be part of the *public*.

Drawing again on Rancière, as the recognition of a subject as a 'political being' goes along with the 'refiguration' of the space he or she belongs to, the juxtaposition of the logics of the camps and the squats becomes more obvious. In fact 'in order to refuse the title of political subjects to a category ... it has traditionally been sufficient to assert that they belong to ... a space separated from public life' (Rancière 2010, 38) – converted in empirical terms, the camp. While, Rancière continues, the politicisation of these categories happens through the re-qualification of those places (the camps), that is 'in getting them to be seen as the spaces of a community, of getting themselves to be seen or heard as speaking subjects (if only in the form of litigation)' (*Ibid.*).

Thus, if migrants are confined in the camps in order to depict them as passive objects of the migration process, within the space of the squat the migrant *subject* becomes an active one – a political subject capable of writing a different script: an activist citizen (Isin 2009, 381).

The Greek context

In Greece, the 'refugee crisis' hit an economically distressed country that was itself reacting to a socio–economic crisis. In the following section I briefly describe migrants' situation in Greece after 2015. I then illustrate how the two aforementioned crises intersect in migrants' and Greeks' daily struggle against precarity and austerity measures. Finally, I introduce the Athenian neighbourhood of Exarcheia where the merging of struggles is epitomised in solidarity and self-organised spaces.

The signing of the EU-Turkey deal[3] on 18 March 2016 and the consequent closure of the 'Balkan route' have exacerbated a situation that for migrants was already at a critical point in Greece. Numbers of migrant arrivals from Turkey to Greece had been rising sharply since spring 2015 and more and more refugees head towards the North, crossing the border with Macedonia at Idomeni. After the sealing of the border due to the signing of the deal, more than 62,000 migrants had been stranded across Greece

(UNHCR 2016). A high rate of rejection of asylum applications and the legalisation of deportations back to Turkey were other consequences of the exclusionary politics of oppression perpetrated by the European Union.

The laboratory of post-national border management put in place by the European Union resulted in the production of a *borderscape*, namely, a 'zone in which different temporalities and overlapping emplacements as well as emergent spatial organisations take place' (Perera 2007, 206–207 in Mezzadra and Neilson 2013, 13). The European border regime had the effect of turning Greece into a 'giant holding zone for thousands of migrants and refugees' (Mezzadra 2018, 929; see also Heller and Pezzani 2016) – a zone scattered with camps and hotspots, materialised in a system that functions as an arbitrary filter for regulating the time and space of migrants' movement in the European territory (Mezzadra and Neilson 2013, 132).

In this sense, Greek camps constitute 'spatial and political formations that blur the boundary between detention facilities and refugee camps across the world' (Mezzadra 2018, 929), and as such they function as a tangible manifestation of power on the lives and bodies of subjects in transit. Migrants are confined in inhumane conditions for an undefined period of time, and transformed into bodies to be cared for, into an indefinite homogeneous category of nameless individuals, denying their decision-making agency and political capacity. This condition is made explicit in the words of a young refugee woman who spent six months in Moria's hotspot in Lesbos before being relocated to Athens, where she lives in a migrant squat.

Moria is a prison within a forest of olive trees. Tall walls, the top of which are barbed. The limit of the camp was 1500 [people], but more than 2000 lived there, with every part crammed full. Those in charge showed an atmosphere of difference and discrimination. They displayed no equality. Different queues and different preferential treatment for different nationalities [...] In Moria, humanity and dignity is a focal question and something one keeps questioning. Often, it's a thing that seems buried under the soil' (Plaza Girls' zine 'The Moria issue').

This description is one of the many that depicts Moria – the biggest hotspot in Greece – as an inhospitable space, where shelters are inadequate for the accommodation of the number of people who are forcibly brought there. Life inside the 'prison' of Moria is characterised by discomfort and danger – women regularly risk physical violence and newborns die from malnutrition or freezing temperatures. Furthermore, human dignity is constantly jeopardised and daily life is marked by discriminatory and racist episodes.

This situation triggered reactions from the solidarity movement that started on the islands and then continued on the mainland, where it joined a broader protest movement against the financial crisis that has affected the country since 2008. When the 'refugee crisis' hit Greece, the country was in a situation of economic distress that caused feelings of anger and uncertainty in a large part of the population. As a reaction to the 'generalised state of exception' that the country was facing since 2008 (Dalakoglou 2013, 35), a powerful social and political movement mobilised in Greece, with actions and demonstrations taking place all around the country – of which the most famous is the occupation of Syntagma square in Athens (see Arampatzi 2017; Dalakoglou and Agelopoulos 2017; Mezzadra 2018).

The occupation of Syntagma square was juxtaposed by a series of spontaneous measures to cope with the humanitarian and political consequences of the crisis. Thousands of people more or less politicised, contributed in the production of adaptive responses and counter-strategies to face the austerity measures and the economic shock, and compensate for the crumbling of the welfare programmes. The resulting urban scenario was scattered with self-organised spaces, social networks and open assemblies that redrew the geography of parts of Athen's city centre (Makrygianni 2017; Vaiou and Kalandides 2017). The autonomous structures and antagonist environment enacted during the crisis prepared a fertile ground for arriving migrants that since the summer 2015 were relocated to Athens from the islands, looking for improvised accommodations in the city. Thousands of migrants who did not end up in the city's camps, settled in squares and public parks, mainly in the area around Victoria square and Pedion tou Areos, in precarious conditions and always exposed to the constant threat of assaults by far-right xenophobic groups. That was the moment when the solidarity movement started mobilising in Athens, with activists offering support to the migrant population in need.

The first migrant squat – Notara 26 – was opened in Athens in September 2015. An abandoned public building became temporary home for around hundred migrants. Notara 26 has been the first of a series of occupations to host migrants, that formed a network of support, politically positioning themselves 'in favour of the "no border" approach, criticising nationalism, patriotism, hierarchies, borders and xenophobia' (Positions Proposal Framework of Antiauthoritarian Movement 2018).[4] After Notara, several buildings were occupied in Athens, mainly located in the neighbourhood of Exarcheia. Exarcheia is a peculiar neighbourhood in the centre of Athens, internationally known as an anarchists and leftists area, whose resistance identity is characterised by the presence of numerous political squats and *aftonoma stekia* (autonomous centres). Solidarity experiences such as self-organised kitchens, healthcare centres, social centres, and community assemblies shape this politically radical urban area, open to inclusion of new subjectivities. The space is characterised by a 'porosity' (Stavrides 2016, 67) that makes it a theatre of expressive acts of encounter and potentially emancipating urban practices. Since 2008, when the still ongoing phase of austerity and neoliberal reform started in Greece, the 'anomic' neighbourhood (Poulimenakos and Dalakoglou 2018) became the headquarter of the solidarity movement in the effort to circulate antagonistic modes of social existence (Kritidis 2014). Generally, the neighbourhood is characterised by a normalisation of more radical tactics, that include occupations of space, riots and use of violence, aimed at creating and preserving what the anarchists call a 'free zone' (free from police and fascists). The access to this space should be granted to anyone, in the sense that everyone – citizen and non – should feel and be safe in this space.

Migrant squats as practices of struggle

> The refugees fought for a life of safety and for their rights, and forced us to take a stand. They sparked an unprecedented solidarity movement. A movement which proved that, even in the depths of crisis, unfairness, fear and racism, the power of solidarity and humanity is still alive. A world of equality and freedom is possible and is in fact being created – we are creating it – in the here and now (City Plaza, flyer for Welcome United action, 2–16 September 2017).

In a supranational space that has been reshaped to make migrants' lives and livelihoods more vulnerable and precarious, both during their travels and in the everyday experiences after crossing the borders, places like Exarcheia materialise as safe havens in a more hostile environment, as spaces where migrants can transit and live freely, and which they can transform according to their needs and ambitions.

While the police, racist and fascist incursions are violently opposed in Exarcheia, the antagonistic practices that take shape in the area often exceed its own physical boundaries. The occupations of migrants are one example of this, as they represent strategies of struggle materialised in a place – but not limited to the site of the particular building – where citizenship is enacted from below. This enactment happens through the appropriation of rights they would not be entitled to according to their legal status, such as the right to move freely, to have access to healthcare and education, and the right to work.

Moreover, migrant squats are places where new subjective relations can happen between migrant and non-migrant activists. It is precisely this dynamic encounter of different activist subjectivities that opens up the analysis to other ways (other then citizenship) of being political, at the same time revealing the limitations of the dichotomous vision of citizens and non-citizens. The contentious politics (Leitner et al. 2008, 157) of resistance they implement through concerted and creative actions, combined with egalitarian practices of solidarity, allows the framing of migrant occupations as spaces of 'autonomous geographies' (Pickerill and Chatterton 2006, 1). In the leftists and libertarian environments, the idea of autonomy is generally associated with a struggle for independence from the capitalist system, negation of power and hierarchy, and self-determination. When referred to migrant practices, the concept becomes even more pivotal since it is the very act of moving (and the decision that implies this act), disconnected from any systemic imposition, that subtends the possibility of developing a new political subjectivity, which is linked to the claiming of rights in a hostile territory (for an extensive analysis of autonomy and migrant squatting see Mudu and Chattopadhyay 2017). Autonomy and the construction of autonomous spaces are also a prerequisite of the social and political project of the Antiauthoritarian Movement (Αντιεξουσιαστική Κίνηση, A.K.) in Greece, one of the most active social movements in Athens. Along with other social movements worldwide, A. K. placed the focus of the struggle on 'the liberation of public space, its reconstruction and its claim as free and social, against the state and capitalist power' (Positions Proposal Framework of Antiauthoritarian Movement 2018). According to the anarchist vision, free public space is conceived as a space of resistance and creation, that can be temporary or permanent. The first category comprises occupied squares and public buildings that, in a given contingency, become centres of struggle for a wider social revolt; while the 'permanent free public spaces' (*Ibidem*) are those free social spaces – either rented or squatted – which are open to everyone, along with squares and neighbourhoods self-organised in permanent assemblies. On this line, migrant squats correspond to the first category, and it is impelling to create 'as many free spaces as possible to break the state of exception' (*Ibidem*). In the words of an activist from Notara 26:

the squat is our community and as much as we have many squats as Notara we create a free zone. A free zone in the centre of the city, with no discrimination, based on self-organisation ... it's our community [...] This free zone, well, it gives a little bit of asylum sometimes, if you want to call it that way – or a sanctuary – because the free zone existed already and we had to create these squats' (anarchist from Notara 26, December 2016).

Nowadays there are eleven migrants' occupations in Athens, in addition to different political spaces and assemblies. Each occupation hosts a number of people ranging from

100 to 200, with approximately 2,000 migrants living in self-managed accommodation spaces. Eight of the migrant squats are located in Exarcheia – Notara 26, Arachovis 44/ 'Single Men' squat, Kaniggos 22, Spyrou Trikoupi 17, Hotel Oniro, 5th School, Clandestina and Themistokleous 58, while the other three – City Plaza, Jasmine School and Acharnon 22 – are in the area surrounding Victoria square.

Although located outside the boundaries of the neighbourhood, these occupations are closely linked to the political groups from which they originate, and along with the other squats are part of a network of mutual support: the Coordination of Refugees Squats assembly (Sintonistikò Prosfigikon Katalipseon). Through this assembly, the squats confront political issues – such as the organisation of demonstrations or other strategies to protect each other in case of fascist attacks or threats of eviction. If a squat has reached its capacity, the activists direct the person or family who could not find accommodation there to another one.

Each occupation is affiliated to pre-existing political groups of the anti-authoritarian and Left-libertarian movement active in the neighbourhood, which organised the opening and supported the daily logistics of most of the squats, at least in their early days. Despite political differences, all the squats reject any form of legal distinction between different reasons for migration, and apply an expansive definition of the term *refugee* that includes people fleeing from war, political persecution, extreme poverty, and environmental devastation.

As stated by the activists, the squats are born and reproduce themselves first as spaces of struggle, in which everyday activities (such as collective decision-making, provision of food and accommodation, site-security, education and health-care) are necessary and collateral to the main political goal. The political stance of the anti-authoritarian movement on this point is clear:

our participation in housing squats was intended, of course, not only to provide physical assistance but also to help with the emergence of different meanings of how we could build communities that include migrants, in order to try and make this new political situation less complex and breaking the state of exception along with migrants (Positions Proposal Framework of Antiauthoritarian Movement 2018).

The rejection of the charity experience is evident, along with the attempt to disrupt the uneven relations of 'guest' and 'host' (Squire and Darling 2013). The occupations perform practices of collective living centered on self-organisation and mutual aid, in which the production and reproduction of free space plays a fundamental role. The creation of such spaces set the ground for the emergence of new possibilities of hybridisation (Mezzadra 2008), perhaps the most significant being the convergence of antagonistic citizens and people in motion united in the same struggle. A writing on a wall in Victoria square epitomises this vision. Appeared in August 2018 (and erased by fascist symbols soon after) the writing invited to join the 'common struggles of migrants and locals', inspiring some of the reflections for this article. Moreover, paraphrasing the slogan of City Plaza squat – 'we live together, we struggle together' – the occupations of migrants and activists foreshadow more meaningful ways of sharing the space and time of everyday life, through the ethical form of cohabitation (Butler 2015). As I will contend later on, this hybridisation does not always happen in a peaceful manner within the newly created groups.

The aspect of cohabitation brings the analysis down to the scale of the inter-personal encounters, and the enrichment this has on the life and memory of the people who inhabit the squats. In fact, the strength of such experiences lies in their capacity to inscribe themselves upon the bodies of the individuals taking part in them, in contrast to the experience in the camps and hotspots which leaves deep emotional and even physical scars in those who experienced those spaces. This does not happen only at a personal level, but also at the level of political confrontation. As in many other cases of autonomous spaces of resistance in Europe and worldwide (Brown and Feigenbaum 2017; Mudu and Chattopadhyay 2017) Athenian migrant squats function as spaces of struggle and challenge exclusionary policies while triggering a subversion of established thresholds between the different subjectivities they enact. With breaking existing barriers individualities meet, producing a new type of hybrid political subjectivity between migrant and non-migrant. In the words of a migrant activist:

as an immigrant anarchist I understand that the struggle for freedom is common between locals and migrants. For this reason I work towards unity and making collective body between locals and migrants. We will not fight only for immigrants but for everyone, because we understand that our pain, our problems are the same (resident of City Plaza, July 2018).

The migrant resident of City Plaza squat underlies his identity as a migrant activist while he makes a clear reference to the merging of struggles between migrants and locals discussed above. Despite the intentions though, the formation of a 'collective body between locals and migrants' is a complex process and not something that should be taken for granted.

As a Greek anarchist declared:

we tried to explain them [the migrants] several times that we are not an NGO [Non Governmental Organisation] and if they don't like it like this they can go ... because we are anarchists and we believe in such values as solidarity and horizontal organisation [...] They come from the experiences of the camps, where they are always told what to do (anarchist from Exarcheia, September 2017).

The anarchist highlights the tensions that exist within the occupations, between migrants and activists themselves. In fact, all the effort aimed at creating communities that include migrants, teaching *them* how to collaborate in an 'anarchist way', betrays a logic of us/them, and imply a vaguely pedagogical approach that in some cases proves necessary for the success of self-management. Even in supposedly non-hierarchical contexts, power asymmetries are difficult to totally eliminate, especially in a situation characterised by temporal precarity and where the subjectivities involved belong to completely different cultural and political contexts.

Access to public space

The geography of the squats in Athens is variable in structures and inhabitants, but stable in its overall political aims. As part of a movement of resistance, migrant squats produce and practice different 'cartographies of belonging' (Turner 2016, 152). These maps are ideally freed from the power relations that subtend the use of space – one of the roots of social power. Within the occupations and in the free space of Exarcheia the use of space by migrants is not put to trial: they do not need to ask for permission (even though they have to comply with anarchist politics). From a political perspective the squats, with their subversive and imaginative power, represent strategies of struggle to gain access to the space of the city. Squats do not merely represent demands for housing or access to welfare, but enact a political agency to gain access to the urban space (Mayer 2012), which it is otherwise denied at a national level: the access to a more abstract political space is strictly linked to the access to the material space of the city. Public space is intended here both in its political and material dimensions, a materially grounded social territory that renders possible interpersonal interactions (Brighenti 2010). Public space is a 'space of intervisibility of subjects' (*Ibidem*, 27) in which social identities interact and define themselves.

Much of the public life in Exarcheia takes place on the street. The streets and the square of Exarcheia are meant to be a safe area for migrants, both for people living in the squats or who come from different parts of the city, often on a daily basis, to attend courses, go to self-managed spaces for medical and legal support, or simply to spend time in a place where they feel safer and more comfortable than in other parts of the city. An important meeting and gathering point, especially for migrants and activists, is Steki Metanaston – Migrants Social Center, Tsamadou 13. Literally 'the gathering of migrants', Steki is a building run by the militants of the political group Diktio, where various activities are organised for and by migrants and asylum seekers – including language courses, book presentations, assemblies and film screenings, while at night it works as a bar with affordable prices. The importance of Steki (and similar places in the neighbourhood, i.e. Nosotros and K*VOX) is to give a sense of normality to the daily life of people who hardly can not have access to other places of leisure, even for mere economic or personal security issues.

Security

Fascist and xenophobic attacks are an issue in Greece in the last years, especially regarding migrants. Both on the islands and in the main cities (i.e. in Thessaloniki, where the squat Libertatia has been burned in January 2018 due to a fascist attack), there have been several episodes of violence explicitly directed towards migrants and their supporters. Athens is no exception (see Bampilis 2017; Triandafyllidou and Kouki 2014). In Exarcheia and in migrant squats safety is another important issue. Each occupation has security at the entrance, and entry to non-residents is allowed only after identification to ensure the safety of the inhabitants, while security plans are in place to react to potential xenophobic attacks and eviction attempts. A 'security team' – consisting of militants and activists belonging to different political groups – has been set up within the neighbourhood, with the aim of reacting in case of dangerous situations, caused by both internal disagreements and external attacks. In some cases, however, the intervention of this 'defense group' has taken ambiguous and conflicting forms, as in the case of the eviction of the Single Men squat in May 2018, which will be discussed later on.

In the most critical cases such as those of the fascist attack with incendiary bombs at Notara 26, a powerful mobilisation took place to make the building habitable again as quickly as possible. Together with the activists, the inhabitants of the neighbourhood also volunteered to help. In an announcement of the squat itself it is highlighted also the importance of support and involvement of the population of the neighbourhood:

after the attack with molotov and gas-bottle bombs the safeguard of the refugees and the assistance of the solidarity acted immediately, using the fire extinguishers of the squat. The over 130 lives that were seriously endangered were saved solely by the immediate reaction of the total of the residents, of the solidarity and the neighbours of the squat.[5]

In other cases, attacks to migrants are initiated by the police. In July 2018, a migrant resident of City Plaza was violently assaulted by the police in Exarcheia, at night and in a liminal area of the neighbourhood. According to his own declaration:

the state by placing permanent police forces in the perimeter of Exarcheia has made a kind of border between us and the rest of Athens, so it is as if they put us in a kind of prison. At the moment we have no other way to resist this prison except riots against the military checkpoints. One of the reasons that the cops wanted to break my wrists is because as they said, I am one of those who participate in the riots (resident of City Plaza, July 2018).

In addition to reporting police violence, in this statement the migrant openly declares his identification as a migrant-activist who participates in the riots. Moreover, this declaration sheds light on the double nature of the neighbourhood. On the one hand, Exarcheia is a safe space whose boundary is theoretically protected; on the other hand, that same boundary works as 'a kind of border' for some of its inhabitants, whose practices and movements are limited in that area of the city.

Along with Exarcheia, the area of Victoria has become an important meeting and gathering place for migrants in the Greek capital since 2015. Although a variety of associations and NGOs are situated around the square, the area is considered particularly unsafe for migrants. The neighbourhood is characterised by a mix of migrants and Greek nationalists: the nearby square of Aghios Panteleimonas was the headquarters of Golden Dawn, and Greek flags are visible in the balconies of many buildings in the area. The dissatisfaction with this forced cohabitation by the Greek nationalists resulted in xenophobic attacks against migrants, which triggered a prompt reaction by solidarity residents, as the creation of a neighbourhood assembly in the squat Villa Amalias in 2014 (Poulimenakos and Dalakoglou 2018).

Ambiguities and contradictions

Narratives about migrant squats often give a romanticised view of the occupations, yielding to the rhetoric of the representation of the 'happy family', even though difficulties and contradictions are an important constitutive part of these experiences.

On the same line, while from an outside gaze Exarcheia appears as a compact and antagonistic political entity, the 'free zone' presents a much more complex geography, composed of different groups with slightly divergent political ideas and aims, which are implemented through sometimes ambiguous practices. For instance, both during open assemblies and in public political statements, some of the political groups in Exarcheia accused one another of attempting to 'impose their authority by military means over self-organised projects [...] acting in the name of social centres and formations of the movement' (Squat Gare statement, 24 May 2017).

As the need for a connection with a political group is fundamental for the opening and management of occupations, it often creates ambiguous situations and difficult political framing. The disagreements and divergences of political strategies within the groups of activists have been projected on the housing occupations of the migrants, turning them in a battlefields to settle antecedent disputes, to which in some cases the migrants take part. These contradictions take place on different levels and in several forms: in the relations between political groups at the level of the neighbourhood, in the connections between activists and migrants or, within the spaces of the squats, triggered by the cohabitation.

Regarding the tensions inside the solidarity movement, one example is provided by the longstanding political disagreement between City Plaza and anarchist groups in Exarcheia. As all the squatted buildings are public ownership, in the case of City Plaza the former hotel is privately owned. The decision of occupying a privately owned building – as well as different political and management strategies that followed the opening – created a tension within the network of migrant squats. The exacerbation of this political divide lead to a temporary suspension of the assembly of the Coordination of Refugees Squats in June 2017.

When it comes to the contradictions between activists and migrants, a striking example is the eviction of the Single Men squat. In May 2018 a group of activists part of the 'security team' violently evacuated the occupation in Arachovis 44, where around 120 men were living, seized most of the inhabitants' property and banned them from returning to the building. In this case, due to the strictly anarchic politics of the activists who squatted the building in the first place, the supporting political group left right after the occupation, and the squat has been eventually entirely (self)managed by the dwellers since the very beginning. The lack of interaction and cooperation with local groups led to a deterioration of the situation inside the squat. Although the official reasons for the eviction were related to the attempt to dismantle the drug dealing in the neighbourhood, the practices that the activists put in place in order to achieve the goal are politically questionable.

Moreover, on a personal level living in a squat might constitute a problem in the already arduous asylum application process. As noted in the case of the City Plaza resident violently assaulted by the police, the fact of living in an occupation can be interpreted in a hostile way by the institutions and this happens also for regulatory procedures. For instance, a migrant resident of City Plaza fears that:

at the interview [for the asylum application procedure] they'll ask me the same questions in different ways for four or five hours, and I have to answer all the times. I need to prove why I cannot stay there, where I come from, and why my family can instead … It will be very difficult … especially because I think the fact that I live in a squat might be a problem when I do the interview, cause they might think that I'm a kind of activist making trouble … But also they have to admit that they were not able to provide another kind of accommodation for me (resident of Plaza, December 2018).

In addition to the fear regarding the outcome of the asylum request procedure, the migrant's words again highlight the inability to provide adequate reception by the institutions. Moreover, even in this case, the migrant identifies himself as a 'kind of activist making trouble' in the eyes of the institutions. Even though in many cases the choice to live in an occupation is an obligatory one, dictated by the extreme living conditions of the camps or on the streets of the city, a migrant living in a squat is an active subject – an activist – who has chosen to opt out of the institutional system (at least temporarily).

Conclusions

Since the exacerbation of the migrants' situation in Greece after the summer of 2015, a powerful solidarity movement mobilised all over the country. This mobilisation has resulted in the occupation of several spaces, to host migrants in dignified conditions.

Drawing on the case of Athens, the experiences of self-organised autonomous reception are interpreted here as strategies of re-appropriation of citizenship rights – of rights entailed in the status of citizen – in opposition to the normative category of the nation-state. The appropriation of citizenship rights is strictly linked to the appropriation of space, intended both as the architectural space of the building, and as the 'liberated public space' of the city (Positions Proposal Framework of the Antiauthoritarian Movement 2018). Migrant squats are considered here as materialisation of both these appropriations, as they constitute instances of migrant activism and resistance to the European border regime rescaled in the urban context.

In the analysis, the space of the squats and the one of the neighbourhood of Exarcheia intertwine and overlap: preserving the 'free zone' is an essential prerequisite for the squats to exist, as for migrants, the neighbourhood is one of the few spaces in the city where they can feel protected and not be stigmatised. Migrant squats deploy their counterpower through their location in the centre of the city also to the extent that 'citizenship is about *being there*' (McNevin 2012, 167; original emphasis): in the squats, migrants are physically *there*, claiming their presence by being visible and audible in the public space of the city.

The space of the squat is formed by a coalition of different subjectivities: the local (and international) activists, mainly belonging to the anti-authoritarian scene, and the migrant activists – a new subjectivity created by the places themselves. The nature of this encounter produces an ambivalent outcome: on the one hand, the aim of the squat is a contingent one: to give a shelter and access to basic welfare to people who would not be entitled otherwise. This puts the experiences of migrant squatting near the framework of the acts of citizenship 'from below' (Nyers and Rygiel 2012). On the other hand, according to their political nature, the subjectivities that compose the squats refuse the sovereignty of the nation-state, and to some extent, also the category of citizenship as formal expression of belonging to a place (McNevin 2012).

Moreover, migrant squats allow a disruptive appearance of equality as through non-hierarchical practices of self-organisation they reject the 'us-them' divide, intrinsic in other forms of reception.

However, these practices are not without contradictions. While the presence of migrants has added new potential to the struggle of anarchists, at the same time the same presence has exacerbated the contradictions that already existed between the different political groups. Moreover, even though the squats could be interpreted as practices of 'rightful presence' as they disrupt the 'host-guest' dymension (Squire and Darling 2013), as can be seen from the interviews, there is always the risk that the power imbalances are not overcome and results in pedagogical practices or instances of welfarism, or worse in decisions such as the eviction of the Single men squat mentioned in the article. The anarchist's pre-existing vision of politics and their ideal strategy to solve the migrant issue do not always meet the demands and desires of migrants. In making the voices of migrants audible, there is an intrinsic asymmetry of power that leads to a risk that the activists reframe those voices according to their external vision and pre-established political expectations. Hybridisation does not always lead to the deconstruction of the 'us-them' divide, and in the merging of the different subjectivities in a unique one. Even though migrants in the squats might perceive themselves as 'activists', a constant renegotiation is necessary between migrants' perspective and the politics of the activists that takes place through daily interactions within the squats and in the neighbourhood.

Even though the political action of migrant squats as a newly formed coalition is concerted through counter-hegemonic and non-hierarchical practices, its participants – migrants and activists – assume different positions within it, due to the different political and social stakes that characterise their presence in the occupations. For the activists/anarchists, the contentious politics of appropriation of space enacted through the squats aim, at the urban scale, to maintain their autonomy from the institutions, at least in the neighbourhood. While, on a transnational scale, migrant squats constitute contingent 'existence strategy' (Sossi 2006) aimed at countering the EU migration policies. On the migrants' side, instead, at stake there is their possibility to move – their 'right to escape' (Mezzadra 2004) – together with their everyday struggle for survival. The autonomy from the system craved by the anarchists is for the migrants an autonomy to move, both in the space of the city and across borders.

Notes

1. Migrants in transit through Greece are directed to other European countries and, according to the Dublin Regulation, being identified would imply the risk of being transferred back to Greece. For this reason, many choose not to be identified and not to start the asylum application process in the country.
2. The hotspots are part of the system of devices created by the European Union to control the flow of migrants and to make a first selection of incoming migrants. On their arrival to the European shores, migrants are taken to those centres (located near landing areas in Greece and Italy), fingerprinted and registered, and subsequently categorised as 'category 1' or asylum seeker (liable to relocation), or 'category 2', irregular access. For its function of an arbitrary filter, the hotspot is seen here as a way to overcome the rule of law and suspend International Refugee Law.
3. The agreement between European Union and Turkey declares Turkey as a safe country for refugees and allows Greece to return to Turkey all the 'irregular' migrants arriving in the country after 20 March 2016.
4. www.antiauthoritarian.gr.
5. https://en.squat.net/2016/08/27/athens-announcement-of-squat-notara-26-about-the-attack-of-august-24th/.

Disclosure statement

No potential conflict of interest was reported by the author.

References

Anderson, B., N. Sharma, and C. Wright. 2012. "'We are All Foreigners'. No Borders as a Practical Political Project." In *Citizenship, Migrant Activism and the Politics of Movement*, edited by P. Nyers and K. Rygiel, 73–91. Abingdon: Routledge.

Arampatzi, A. 2017. "Contentious Spatialities in an Era of Austerity: Everyday Politics and 'Struggle Communities' in Athens, Greece." *Political Geography* 60: 47–56. doi:10.1016/j.polgeo.2017.03.010.

Avallone, G. 2018. *Liberare Le Migrazioni: Lo Sguardo Eretico Di Abdelmalek Sayad*. Verona: Ombre Corte.

Bampilis, T. 2017. "Far-Right Extremism in the City of Athens during the Greek Crisis." In *Critical Times in Greece: Anthropological Engagements with the Crisis*, edited by D. Dalakoglou and G. Agelopoulos, 59–72. London: Routledge.

Brighenti, A. 2010. "The Publicness of Public Space: On the Public Domain." Quaderno 49, University of Trento http://eprints.biblio.unitn.it/1844/

Brown, G., and A. Feigenbaum, eds. 2017. *Protest Camps in International Context: Spaces, Infrastructures and Media of Resistance*. Bristol: Policy Press.

Butler, J. 2015. *Notes toward a Performative Theory of Assembly*. Cambridge: Harvard University Press.

Dadusc, D., and P. Mudu. 2019. "Care without Control? The Criminalisation of Migrants Solidarity and the Humanitarian Industrial Complex." *Geopolitics* (forthcoming).

Dalakoglou, D. 2013. "The Crisis before "The Crisis": Violence and Urban Neoliberalization in Athens." *Social Justice* 39 (1): 24–42.

Dalakoglou, D., and G. Agelopoulos. eds. 2017. *Critical Times in Greece: Anthropological Engagements with the Crisis*. London: Routledge.

Darling, J. 2017a. "Forced Migration and the City: Irregularity, Informality, and the Politics of Presence." *Progress in Human Geography* 41 (2): 178–198. doi:10.1177/0309132516629004.

Darling, J. 2017b. "Acts, Ambiguities, and the Labour of Contesting Citizenship." *Citizenship Studies* 21 (6): 727–736. doi:10.1080/13621025.2017.1341658.

De Genova, N. 2015. "Border Struggles in the Migrant Metropolis." *Nordic Journal of Migration Research* 5 (1): 3–10. doi:10.1515/njmr-2015-0005.

Depraetere, A., and S. Oosterlynck. 2017. "'I Finally Found My Place': A Political Ethnography of the Maximiliaan Refugee Camp in Brussels." *Citizenship Studies* 21 (6): 693–709. doi:10.1080/13621025.2017.1341653.

Garelli, G., and M. Tazzioli. 2013. "Challenging the Discipline of Migration: Militant Research in Migration Studies, an Introduction." *Postcolonial Studies* 16 (3): 245–249. doi:10.1080/13688790.2013.850041.

Grazioli, M. 2017. "From Citizens to Citadins? Rethinking Right to the City inside Housing Squats in Rome, Italy." *Citizenship Studies* 21 (4): 393–408. doi:10.1080/13621025.2017.1307607.

Harvey, D. 2012. *Rebel Cities: From the Right to the City to the Urban Revolution*. London: Verso books.

Heller, C., and L. Pezzani 2016. "Ebbing and Flowing: The EU's Shifting Practices of (Non-) Assistance and Bordering in a Time of Crisis." *Near Futures Online* 1:1. http://nearfuturesonline.org/ebbing-and-flowing-the-eus-shifting-practices-of-non-assistance-and-bordering-in-a-time-of-crisis/

Hindess, B. 2004. "Citizenship for All." *Citizenship Studies* 8 (3): 305–315. doi:10.1080/1362102042000257023.

Isin, E. F. 2009. "Citizenship in Flux: The Figure of the Activist Citizen." *Subjectivity* 29 (1): 367–388. doi:10.1057/sub.2009.25.

Kotronaki, L. 2018. "Outside the Doors: Refugee Accommodation Squats and Heterotopy Politics." *South Atlantic Quarterly* 117 (4): 914–924. doi:10.1215/00382876-7166080.

Kritidis, G. 2014. "The Rise and Crisis of the Anarchist and Libertarian Movement in Greece, 1973–2012." In *The City Is Ours: Squatting and Autonomous Movements in Europe from the 1970s to the Present*, edited by B. Van der Steen, A. Katzeff, and L. van Hoogenhuijze, 63–94. Oakland: PM Press.

Lafazani, O. 2018. "Homeplace Plaza: Challenging the Border between Host and Hosted." *South Atlantic Quarterly* 117 (4): 896–904. doi:10.1215/00382876-7166043.

Lefebvre, H. 1974. *The Production of Space*. Oxford: Blackwell.

Leitner, H., E. Sheppard, and K. M. Sziarto. 2008. "The Spatialities of Contentious Politics." *Transactions of the Institute of British Geographers* 33 (2): 157–172. doi:10.1111/j.1475-5661.2008.00293.x.

Maestri, G., and S. Hughes. 2017. "Contested Spaces of Citizenship: Camps, Borders and Urban Encounters." *Citizenship Studies*. doi:10.1080/13621025.2017.1341657.

Makrygianni, V. 2017. "Migrant Squatters in the Greek Territory Practices of Resistance and the Production of the Athenian Urban Space." In *Migration, Squatting and Radical Autonomy*, edited by P. Mudu and S. Chattopadhyay, 248–256. London: Routledge.

Mayer, M. 2012. "The "Right to the City" in Urban Social Movements." In *Cities for People, Not for Profit*, edited by N. Brenner, P. Marcuse, and M. Mayer, 75–97. London: Routledge.

McNevin, A. 2012. "Undocumented Citizens? Shifting Grounds of Citizenship in Los Angeles." In *Citizenship, Migrant Activism and the Politics of Movement*, edited by P. Nyers and K. Rygiel, 165–183. Abingdon: Routledge.

Mezzadra, S. 2004. "The Right to Escape." *Ephemera* 4 (3): 267–275.

Mezzadra, S. 2008. *La Condizione Postcoloniale: Storia E Politica Nel Presente Globale*. Verona: Ombre corte.

Mezzadra, S. 2011. "The Gaze of Autonomy: Capitalism, Migration and Social Struggles." In *The Contested Politics of Mobility: Borderzones and Irregularity*, edited by V. Squire, 121–142. Basingstoke: Palgrave Macmillan.

Mezzadra, S. 2018. "In the Wake of the Greek Spring and the Summer of Migration." *South Atlantic Quarterly* 117 (4): 925–933. doi:10.1215/00382876-7166092.

Mezzadra, S., and B. Neilson. 2013. *Border as Method, Or, the Multiplication of Labor*. Durham and London: Duke University Press.

Mudu, P., and S. Chattopadhyay, eds. 2017. *Migration, Squatting and Radical Autonomy*. London: Routledge.

Nyers, P., and K. Rygiel, eds. 2012. *Citizenship, Migrant Activism and the Politics of Movement*. London: Routledge.

Oikonomakis, L. 2018. "Solidarity in Transition: The Case of Greece". In *Solidarity Mobilizations in the 'Refugee Crisis'*, edited by D. Della Porta, 65–98. Basingstoke: Palgrave Macmillan.

Papdopoulos, D., and V. Tsianos. 2007. "How to Do Sovereignty without People? the Subjectless Condition of Postliberal Power." *Boundary 2: International Journal of Literature and Culture* 34 (1): 135–172. doi:10.1215/01903659-2006-030.

Perera, S. 2007. "A Pacific zone? (In) security, sovereignty, and stories of the Pacific borderscape". In *Borderscapes: Hidden Geographies and Politics and Territory's Edge*, edited by Rajaram, P. K., and Grundy-Warr, C., 201–227. Minneapolis: University of Minnesota Press.

Pickerill, J., and P. Chatterton. 2006. "Notes Towards Autonomous Geographies: Creation, Resistance and Self-Management as Survival Tactics." *Progress in Human Geography* 30 (6): 730–746. doi:10.1177/0309132506071516.

Poulimenakos, G., and D. Dalakoglou. 2018. "Hetero-Utopias: Squatting and Spatial Materialities of Resistance at Times of Crisis in Athens." In *Critical Times in Greece: Anthropological Engagements with the Crisis*, edited by D. Dalakoglou and G. Agelopoulos, 173–187. London: Routledge.

Raimondi, V. 2019. "Resisting the Camp: Migrants' Squats as Antithetical Spaces in Athens's City Plaza." In *Sanctuary Cities and Urban Struggles. Rescaling Migration, Citizenship, and Rights*, edited by J. Darling and H. Bauder, 191–216. Manchester: Manchester University Press.

Rancière, J. 1995. *On the Shores of Politics*. London: Verso.

Rancière, J. 1999. *Disagreement*. Minnesota: University of Minnesota Press.

Rancière, J. 2010. *Dissensus on Politics and Aesthetics*. London: Continuum.

Sayad, A. 1999. *La Double Absence. Des Illusions De L'émigré Aux Souffrances De L'immigré*. Paris: Éditions du Seuil.

Sossi, F. 2006. *Migrare. Spazi Di Confinamento E Strategie Di Esistenza*. Milano: Il Saggiatore.

Squire, V. 2016. *The Exclusionary Politics of Asylum*. Basingstoke: Palgrave Macmillan.

Squire, V., and J. Darling. 2013. "The "Minor" Politics of Rightful Presence: Justice and Relationality in City of Sanctuary." *International Political Sociology* 7 (1): 59–74. doi:10.1111/ips.2013.7.issue-1.

Stavrides, S. 2016. *Common Space. The City as Commons*. London: Zed Books.

Triandafyllidou, A., and H. Kouki. 2014. "Naturalizing Racism in the Center of Athens in May 2011: Lessons from Greece." *Journal of Immigrant & Refugee Studies* 12 (4): 418–436. doi:10.1080/15562948.2014.932477.

Turner, J. 2016. "(En) Gendering the Political: Citizenship from Marginal Spaces." *Citizenship Studies* 20 (2): 141–155. doi:10.1080/13621025.2015.1132569.

UNCHR 2016. "Refugee/Migrants Emergency Response – Mediterranean."Accessed 20 May 2019. https://data2.unhcr.org/en/situations/mediterranean?id=83

Vaiou, D., and A. Kalandides. 2017. "Practices of Solidarity in Athens: Reconfigurations of Public Space and Urban Citizenship." *Citizenship Studies* 21 (4): 440–454. doi:10.1080/ 13621025.2017.1307605.

Urban commons and freedom of movement: the housing struggles of recently arrived migrants in Rome

Nicola Montagna and Margherita Grazioli

ABSTRACT
The arrival of migrants on Italian coasts following the so-called Arab Spring in 2011 has led to a multiplication of housing struggles. These struggles are widespread across the country and focus on the occupation of abandoned buildings and their transformation into collective housing spaces to provide an alternative to the formal reception system. This article will focus on the housing struggles in Rome, as the place with the highest number of occupations and the longest tradition of campaigns for the right to housing of migrants in the country. These struggles are the outcome of the encounter of recently arrived migrants with local solidarity movements and build on existing occupation movements and housing struggles. The article explores how the mobilizations over the right to housing intersect with issues such as the social appropriation of urban commons, the regeneration from below of unused areas, freedom of movement, and the contestation of Italian government policies on the relocation of migrants and refugees. The paper argues that housing struggles not only appropriate and regenerate urban commons, but also challenge the reception governance of migration and the policies of border control.

Introduction

On 6 September 2018 Italian news reported that 51 migrants, mainly from Eritrea, vanished from two reception centres run by the Catholic church organisation Caritas. They were among the 144 migrants who were stranded at sea on the coastguard ship *Diciotti* for ten days in August 2018 as a result of the minister of interior Salvini's refusal to allow the vessel to dock at the Sicilian port of Catania. As the director of Caritas Italiana, don Francesco Soddu, pointed out, this was a 'voluntary departure, not an escape,' as 'nobody wants to stay in Italy' (La Repubblica 2018a). The 'departure' did not last long. The police in Ventimiglia found 34 migrants at the border between Italy and France, a further 17 were tracked down by the police at Baobab Experience, an informal tent camp near the train station Tiburtina in Rome. The 51 migrants were just a few of the nearly 500,000 who arrived in Italy to seek asylum and a better life between 2015 and 2018 and the nearly 200,000 who refused to be stranded in the Italian reception system and the patronising assistance of the state. Thousands of people have, in fact, either relocated themselves and moved to other European countries through 'secondary movements' or stayed in Italy outside the formal reception system. It has been calculated that more than 10,000 of the recent arrivals live in squats, informal settlements or camps while many thousands of others pass through these before moving to Europe (Frontiere 2016, 3).

This paper argues that squatted areas and spaces can become urban commons that facilitate migrants'[1] autonomy in moving and settling across the cityscape and borders. At first, freedom of movement[2] and squatting for housing purposes may seem to belong to different conceptual leagues of the urban experience, since they allude respectively to movement and settlement. Nevertheless, we argue that these two aspects are not mutually exclusive. On the contrary, they represent two intertwining spatial and temporal articulations of the recent migration; while occupations represent the refusal of state-led relocation and mobility policies, they also claim the right to housing. In order to substantiate this argument, we look at some emblematic moments and sites of housing struggles in Rome where recently arrived migrants have been the protagonists.

Our core argument is that, while the wave of squatting involving the migrants who arrived after the Arab spring and during the border regime crisis is a response to multiple crises – the crisis of the reception system, the humanitarian crisis, the housing crisis in some metropolitan areas including Rome – it is also a practical contestation of border policies through movement containment, and a form of urban commoning through participatory practices by the occupiers (Bollier 2015; Micciarelli 2017). On the one hand, squatting of urban areas responds to the housing needs of those migrants who are not in reception – either because they have never entered or have been expelled from the system. Since these people cannot access the privatised housing market because of status or income limitations, squatting is often the only option they have left. On the other hand, the growth of informal settlements outside the reception system also questions the legitimacy of moving people through resettlement schemes according to bureaucratic, security and labour-market related criteria (De Genova 2017; Fontanari and Ambrosini 2018; Picozza 2017).

While reception in principle is designed to facilitate migrants' transition into the receiving society by equipping them with the skills and knowledge needed for long-term, self-sufficient integration (Blitz et al. 2017), the practice is rather different. With its rules tying individuals to a specific location, reception is a 'practice of bordering' (Yuval Davis, Wemyss, and Cassidy 2018) that aims to contain mobility and reinstate border controls within the Italian territory (Pinelli 2016, 2017; Tazzioli 2014). It is a system producing 'immobile subjects' (Borri 2017), people who are stuck to a place they do not choose with little freedom of movement. Rather than promoting inclusion, the reception system regulates mobility, contributing to the strengthening of borders.

In this context of *unwanted* immobility (Conlon 2011) migrant housing struggles become a challenge to this policy of containment of movement. The squatting of former estates, car parks, factories, hotels and offices happens in several Italian towns, as a response to the housing needs of people who are pushed out of, or decide to opt out of, the reception system and its corresponding fostered housing. In cities like Rome, these forms of informal settlement add to and mix with the consolidated practice of squatting that urban social movements enact to repossess and proliferate manifold forms of urban commons, housing included (Squatting Europe Kollective 2014; Bresnihan and Byrne 2014). As we will see in the empirical section of this article, some forms of squatting and informal settlement are intended only to provide emergency shelter to people in conditions of severe housing deprivation. Others are supported by activist networks who share their toolbox of care, political and organisational practices. The latter forms configure 'commoning' efforts in contrast with a static, juridical understanding of 'common' (see the next section and De Angelis in this Special Issue).

Migrants' forms of autonomous settlement constitute a demand for autonomy and emancipation that exceeds the limitations of the current governance of internal and external borders, which is still designed for a mechanical, 'flux-based' understanding of mobility. The argument that squats, urban camps and informal settlements represent mobile and urban commons enabling migrants' autonomy is foregrounded by the empirical materials collected in three of these sites: Quattro Stelle Occupato, Baobab Experience, and the former Penicillina Leo. Based on these cases, we seek to contribute to the burgeoning debate about the commons and its conceptual as well as its tangible constitution (Bailey and Mattei 2013; De Angelis 2017; Mattei 2011; Papadopoulos and Tsianos 2013). In particular, this article draws on in-depth semi-structured interviews with migrant and Italian squatters, solidarity activists and members of NGOs, and on observational ethnographic work in the areas of the three case studies analysed here. The fieldwork was carried out between November 2014 and May 2018.

Moving beyond the economic-juridical dichotomy, we look at the commons in terms of social practices based on mutuality, solidarity, care and decommodified exchange that aims to facilitate migrants' autonomous mobility and settlement. We also identify differences in terms of commoning between these experiences and show that not all the three occupations have been turned into urban commons. Moreover, while we are aware that migration policies, economic contingencies, political instabilities and environmental disasters play a huge role in people's decision to move, this contribution investigates mobility in its irreducibility to external forces.

The paper is organised in three sections. In the first, we review the main coordinates in the debate about the commons. This is functional for including autonomous forms of inhabitancy in the category of the urban commons, the processual transformation of space and social reproduction realised by subjects who do not rely on formal status to claim their autonomy. The second section clarifies the historical and contemporary connection between migration and self-made housing in Rome. The third section draws on the authors' fieldwork in Rome regarding the cases of a housing squat (4 Stelle Occupato), an urban camping (Baobab Experience) and an informal settlement (the former Penicillina Leo) to present the conditions of possibility and limitations under which self-constructed, squatted spaces can configure mobile (Papadopoulos and Tsianos 2013) and urban commons inside cities.

Commons vs commoning

The expanding debate on the commons relates to those material and immaterial resources that should be subtracted from commodification and privatisation and be preserved for common use. The debate has tried not only to define the realm of what is common(s), but also the formal enfranchisement required to facilitate access to these resources. As such, the dichotomy between ownership and right-to-use is a cardinal one in the contemporary debate. This section summarises the theoretical trends of the debate on the commons, identifying three main approaches: the Anglophone, which emphasises the indivisibility of the commons; the continental, which focuses on the commons as rights; and a third way, which investigates the commons in terms of commoning and social practices. This brief discussion will allow us to qualify housing squats and informal settlements as urban commons and situate our contribution through the empirical analysis of three cases in Rome. Our standpoint is that recent housing struggles expand the existing debate about the commons, where squatting practices trump the dichotomy between 'private' and 'public'. In addition, we argue, migrants' practices of squatting and informal settlement bridge the conceptualisation of urban commons and that of mobile commons since they can configure forms of life in common and the re-appropriation of space, and foster freedom of movement and settlement against exploitative and constraining border regimes.

In the last decade or so Italy has witnessed significant mobilisations, both at a national level and at a regional and urban scale, with a variety of collective actors framing them in terms of commons movements. On 12 June 2011 nearly 26 million people, 95 percent of voters, opposed the privatisation of water in the referendum for 'water as commons' (Bailey and Mattei 2013; Carrozza and Fantini 2016). In early 2011 the main metalworkers' union, FIOM (Federazione Impiegati ed Operai Metalmeccanici – the union of blue- and white-collar metalworkers), organised a major demonstration under the slogan 'labour is a common.' For more than 20 years the NO TAV movement has protested against the 56 kilometre-long tunnel holing the Alps between Turin and Lyon and in defence of the local environment as a common (Centro sociale Askatasuna 2013). On 15 April and 14 June 2011, the Teatro Palazzo and Teatro Valle in Rome were occupied and declared a common (Aa.Vv. 2012). These occupations generated a wide debate on 'culture as a common', which found a resonance in the 2012 mass student protests that claimed the 'university as a common' against cuts to the education system. Finally, there has also been a growing interest in the urban dimension of commons in the context of recent collective struggles against the privatisation of resources, services and the 'new urban enclosures' (Hodkinson 2012, see also Montagna 2006) as a means of creating alternative forms of communal life and economic and social reproduction in times of economic crisis (Grazioli 2018). As a consequence of these mobilisations, the institutional incorporation of the commons by political parties and in the governance of cities is not a surprise (Bianchi 2018).

These different ways of looking at the commons and adapting this concept to different goods reflect the theoretical debate, which has also articulated this concept in diverse ways. In Anglophone countries, an economic meaning has traditionally prevailed whereby commons are understood as indivisible goods, in the sense that no one has an exclusive right to them, such as land, water and forests, which should be shared and managed by the community (Hardin 1968; Ostrom 1990). These are natural resources that have the characteristics of being *places of non-right*, where individuals as private actors are not entitled to have rights. Drawing on Ostrom's work, Joan Subirats (2012) defines the commons as those 'goods and resources that, rather than being bound by ideas of property or belonging, assume by their own natural and economic vocation functions of social interest, serving the interest not of public administration but those of a given collectivity and the people who make it up'.

Commons are goods that belong to collectivities and local communities. Their specific status does not respond to the binary logic of public and private property that has dominated the economic, social and political debate. According to the economic approach, commons are a given priority: some goods have this character because of their function within a community. In Mediterranean countries including Italy and Spain, where this debate is linked to collective mobilisations, a juridical and political definition by which commons – 'beni comuni' in Italian, 'común' in Spanish – are interpreted in terms of public utilities the use of which should be guaranteed as a right to each individual regardless of their gender, class or nationality. Consequently, the reproduction of these commons should be preserved from capitalist enclosure and commodification that would deteriorate their quality, openness and accessibility. Along these lines, water, air, forests and woodlands but also human artefacts (i.e. archaeological and cultural environments), represent commons, which, as described by the Rodotà commission, are 'goods whose utility is functional to the pursuit of fundamental rights and free development of the person (...) The legal title to the commons can be held by private individuals, legal persons or by public entities. No matter their title, *their collective fruition must be safeguarded*, within the limits of and according to the process of law'.

Although this formulation lists a number of diverse physical goods, the emphasis is on their aims. Commons are means to an end, they are functional to the achievement of the full development of individual. Commons are the condition through which new relationships between individuals can be established that are mediated neither by the state nor the market. They can belong to private individuals and still be *fruited* by collectivities outside the rules of the market. In a further but related development, Mattei 2012) view of the commons as is different from the individualistic vision as conceived by the capitalist tradition, taking everyone's equal right to access as the starting point. The commons cannot be commodified (because they cannot be transferred, or alienated), and they cannot be the object of individualised and exclusive possession. Thus, they express a logic that is qualitative, not a quantitative; relational, not exclusive. We do not 'have' a common good, we 'form part of' the common good, in that we form part of an ecosystem, a system of relations in an urban or rural environment. The notion of commons as developed by Italian jurists such as Rodotà and Mattei rejects the essentialist and naturalistic idea of commons. Rather, they are regarded as historically and socially constructed in relation to the foundation of the constitutional order of a country. As a consequence, this approach does not simply establish an association between fundamental rights and common goods, but rather sees commons as produced through fundamental rights.

A third approach considers the commons as a process of the creation of social reproductive and organisational forms. In this paper, we understand migrants' squatting and informal settlements as parts of the process of commoning whenever they manage to consolidate 'values practices and measures that are truly alternative to the subordination of life to profit (...). Values practices, such as loyalty to friends, conviviality, mutual aid, care, and even struggles, are developed in the commons' (De Angelis 2017, 12). These practices represent commoning which redefines ownership as 'based on human deeds not property deeds' (Linebaugh 2008: 45), as when migrants squat and inhabit unused urban spaces to satisfy social necessities that are not profitable to, nor consented to by, the formal owner. Hence, these empirical articulations bridge the theoretical definitions of the urban commons and mobile commons, since they both rely on commoning processes that consolidate new spatial, political and social relations in order to maintain and reproduce themselves inside the urban fabric (Grazioli 2017).

In summary, the approach we adopt in this paper in framing housing squats and informal settlements challenges the dichotomy between private and public that under-pins the juridical, economic and environmental approach to the commons, which is concerned with the property entitlement to goods such as water, land, urban heritage etc., and therefore with who is formally enfranchised to benefit from them. Indeed, urban commons such as housing squats and informal settlements are not ruled accord-ing to a formal entitlement to use and ownership based on their consolidated fruitful-ness for collectivities. As such, they are not constituted as 'commons', either in the *de jure* or *de facto* form. *Being* common is not an ontological characteristic of urban squats as it may be for other resources like water or the environment. Neither is it a legal status, as the spaces are usually privately-owned and therefore governed by private property rights. They may *become* commons when this quality is generated by the social practices involved in them, beyond the repossession and illegal use of space. Lastly, their connection to the interplay of autonomy and coercion can represent a point of their coalescence or make them more ephemeral and subject to precarity and forcible dissolution.

All these elements will be discussed empirically, starting from a contextualisation of the relation between mobility and self-made forms of inhabitancy in Rome, in order to discuss how these can constitute urban and mobile commons, enabling the settlement and mobility of migrants in the Italian capital city.

Migration and self-made inhabitancy in rome

Squatting and self-made housing are ingrained in Rome's fabric as a self-made city (Cellamare 2014), developed in the field of tension among institutional planning, capitalist land-grabbing and the grassroots actions developed after the Second World War by different collective actors to demand decent and affordable accommodation (Davoli 2019). Housing rights movements and trade unions mobilised the demands of internal migrants and shanty-town inhabitants. These organisations became, from the 1970s, propellers of social mobilisations concerned with rights and access to the urban and political spaces of welfare, starting with the right to housing (S.M.U.R 2014; Grazioli 2017). Regardless of the permanent demand for social and affordable housing, the last public plans date back to the Petroselli city council at the end of the 1970s. Hence, changing migration patterns intersected with increasingly restrictive access to welfare provision (public housing included) and the widespread commodification of the housing market, which is currently the main legal housing provider in Rome (Gentili and Hoekstra 2018). As a result, migrants were disproportionately affected by patterns of housing segregation and marginalisation, which further reinforced a spatial distribu-tion bound to family and community ties, the local labour and housing market, the attitudes of residents and local governmental actors (Mudu 2006).

As a result, since the 1980s, 'international' migrants started to populate the urban borderlands. They adopted self-made urbanism as a viable option for accessing inhabitancy while emancipating themselves from market-based and/or institutional constraints (S.M.U. R 2014). The paramount example of this is the former Pantanella pasta factory located in the Prenestino-Labicano neighbourhood, which was squatted between August 1990 and January 1991 by about 3,000 migrants, mostly of Asian and North African origin (see De

Angelis 1991). Since the 1990s studies concerned with squatting have focused their analyses on overtly political and anti-capitalist forms of squatting such as social centres (Squatting Europe Kollective 2014), whilst self-made housing was downplayed as essentially deprivation-based practice (Pruijt 2013), especially when carried out by migrants. However, the presence of migrants and their enactment of self-made housing is relevant not only for the change they represented in the ethnic and social composition of squatters in Rome, but also for the contentious politics, organisational practices and *meticcia* (mixed) social reproduction that they established (Grazioli 2018). The centrality of migrants' self-made housing was returned to the centre of the political arena by the so-called Tsunami Tours (Armati 2015) – simultaneous rounds of squatting coordinated by housing rights movements that increased the number of buildings squatted in Rome to approximately 80 (Regione Lazio 2014). Of these, 64 are used for habitation and 55 are affiliated to the main housing rights organisations Blocchi Precari Metropolitani, Coordinamento Cittadino di Lotta per la Casa, ASIA USB and Action (Nur and Sethman 2017; Davoli 2019). Those buildings that remain unaffiliated tend to replicate similar modalities of internal self-management, besides occasionally taking part in political mobilisations (as was the case with the Via Curtatone, inhabited mostly by refugees and evicted in summer 2017). Lastly, there is the 'typology' of informal settlement and urban camps which are often elusive to official mapping due to their 'invisibility', lack of political organisation or precariousness due to evictions and displacement. According to estimates by the city council and builders' associations, some 12,000 people are currently squatting for housing purposes (La Repubblica 2018b) and roughly 70–80 percent of squatters are migrants of differing status. The majority are from North and Central Africa (in particular Tunisia and Morocco), Central and South America (Ecuador and Peru) and Eastern Europe (Ukraine and Romania). Most arrived after the Arab Spring or during the last few years. Based on this historic and contemporary relation between self-made forms of inhabitancy and mobility in Rome, we will now move on to discuss how the right to housing in Rome has intersected with transnational mobility and internal border management.

Migrant housing struggles and reception policy in rome

As previously outlined, the connection between migration and informal modalities of inhabitancy is ingrained in Rome's housing history. Nevertheless, the controversial issues – and therefore demands – in this struggle have gained a transnational relevance since Rome became the point of encounter, transit and eventually settlement of thousands of migrants who arrived on Italy's Southern coasts. This section focuses on three examples of the most visible forms of current settlement in the city that are alternatives to 'mainstream' forms of housing, including those provided by the reception system: organised housing squats, urban camping and informal settlements. Although they are separated here for analytical purposes, they share similar features in terms of social composition of the occupants and have common political demands and joint mobilisations – the latter activated especially over specific policy and governance ruptures, such as the crackdown on evictions, restrictive borders and urban space policing. This said, the purpose of this section is to highlight how these forms of inhabitancy are articulated in relation to migration, creating politics of affection, solidarity networks and actions that configure commons, enable processes of commoning and challenge the strengthening of internal borders by containing free movement. These developments are generated through the reception of migrants outside the formal system and the provision of information and resources that free them from the constraints of containment policies and facilitate their movement; and through the everyday effort of cooperating towards the transformation of the squatted space in liveable ones, maintaining them, and creating collective forms of daily life. These case studies highlight the conditions of possibility that underpin the constitution of these self-made forms of inhabitancy as urban and mobile commons within Rome's borderscapes.

4 Stelle occupato: commoning housing occupations through solidarity practices

The former 4 Stelle Eurostar Congress, located at Via Prenestina 944, was occupied on 6 December 2012 by hundreds of people in a condition of severe housing deprivation under the lead of the organisation Blocchi Precari Metropolitani (Metropolitan Precarious Block, hereafter BPM). The group of activists supports the internal self-organisation of the squat according to consensus-based plural decision-making, while guaranteeing its inclusion within the mobilisations of housing rights movements (Mudu 2014; Nur and Sethman 2017). Today, the squat houses roughly 500 people (141 of whom are minors) distributed in 140 'nuclei familiari' (households). This terminology, breaking with a heteronormative definition of 'family', indicates BPM's political posture towards a process of building community based on solidarity and mutualism through the creation of autonomous infrastructures that support everyday social reproduction as well as contentious politics for the 'right to the city' (Grazioli and Caciagli 2018). In particular, the squat's cardinal organisational rites (Grazioli 2018) are represented by assembly-based decision making, egalitarian distribution of housing units, collective management of communal spaces (i.e. the former congress hall, restaurant and gym), anti-eviction defence, and participation in the mobilisations promoted by the housing rights movements. BPM squatters implemented further activities such as after school childcare, movie screenings and sport activities (i.e. boxing clubs). Moreover, the peculiar trajectory of the building, its location in a peripheral area and the size of the squatter population have raised public and media interest – for example, a crew of independent filmmakers created a web-doc narrating in slow motion the daily social reproduction of the squatters from early morning to evening, from the squat's picketing to collective childcare (Paolo Palermo and Valerio Muscella 2014). All these activities fostered networking with the surrounding neighbourhood of Tor Sapienza and other grassroots community groups rooted in the area of Roma Est, beyond the established network of housing squats and BPM's political alliances (Grazioli 2017).

Within this framework, the relevance of mobility and migration for the modalities of internal organising and political mobilisation that 4 Stelle's inhabitants have adopted with BPM activists' cooperation since occupying the building is ingrained in the squat's social composition as well as in the squatters' individual biographies. First of all, the vast majority of the squatters are migrants with differentiated statuses, ethnic and migratory backgrounds. Among them, many decided to live in a housing squat after they were pushed out or decided to opt out of the formalised reception system, as attested to by the MSF report *Fuori Campo* (2016).[3] Abdul.,[4] 30 years old, is a Sudanese refugee who, on arrival in Italy, was institutionalised for two years in the reception system. Thereafter, his trajectory included periods dwelling in housing squats, such as the former Hotel Africa, as well as transit through reception centres such as the one allocated to the Sudanese community in Via di Scorticabove, run by a privatised contractor. He finally decided to move into the 4 Stelle Occupato (where two of his children were born) because he could not live in the centre with his wife. As he stated: '[they][5] were treating us like babies who cannot cook, work, watch for ourselves; we are just business to them, yet we don't want to be. We want to have our job, our families, our independence.'[6] From his perspective, the 4 Stelle was his chance to emancipate himself from an infantilising system, while creating networks of care with, and for, fellow squatters and with other urbanites living in Rome without any solidarity or community network (Papadopoulos 2018). In addition, the 4 Stelle 'absorbed' the evictees of other housing squats and informal settlements, including Piazza Indipendenza and Via di Scorticabove, which was evicted on administrative grounds in summer 2018. H. and other squatters, together with families and friends, also participated in the anti-racist mobilisations that followed the rise of migrant deaths in the Mediterranean Sea, as in the case of the April 2015 shipwreck (Grazioli 2018).

Baobab experience: mobile spaces, mobile commons

The urban camping Baobab Experience originated from the former reception centre Baobab, evicted in 2015 after license was withdrawn following the *Mafia Capitale* scandal, a case of corruption that involved the city council in the 2000s. The camp has moved around different areas adjacent to the Tiburtina railway station, which is a meeting point for many homeless or travelling people, migrants included, and has undergone more than 20 evictions, the final one on 10 November 2018. The most durable camping site was Piazzale Maslax, named by the activists in memory of a migrant who lived at Baobab Experience for a few weeks and took his life in Foggia after being deported from Sweden in compliance with the Dublin rules requiring migrants to live in the country where they were first identified. The camp could host up to 300 people but was mostly a transit site. It is calculated that more than 70,000 migrants passed through the camp. The majority were represented by males aged 20–30, with the main nationalities being Eritrean, Sudanese, Somalian and Iraqi (although there was a huge influx of migrants from other parts of Africa as well as Pakistan, Kurdistan and Afghanistan between 2017 and 2018). The majority of transient migrants had not yet entered the reception system and needed legal advice and support to apply for asylum. They had come straight by bus or train from Sicily and stopped in Rome where they had contacts and hoped to settle – if not in Rome, at least in Italy. Many others refused to be accommodated in one of the hotspots spread all over the country, since identification and fingerprinting would involve being stuck in Italy while waiting for papers. On the other hand, many wanted to attempt moving to other EU countries, even if they lacked contacts or support networks. Given this situation, the function of the Baobab Experience's volunteers was to elucidate the workings of the EU border management system, provide migrants with essential goods (i.e. water, food, clothes) and protection from sleeping rough, as well as medical and legal assistance (for those asylum seekers and visa applicants whose requests had been rejected). Volunteers helped individuals and groups to explore their options, whether they opted for settlement in Italy or decided to relocate elsewhere inside or outside the EU. As one volunteer put it, 'For them [migrants], Baobab is a place to rest before they can continue their journey and it is an opportunity to escape the rules imposed by Dublin and EU policies' (Gigliola, Baobab Experience activist). Others 'do not know exactly what to do, and need to spend some time in Rome until they make a decision over the direction to take' (Serena, Baobab Experience activist).

This activism was also meant to tackle the threat of deportation and exploitation in informal economies (such as agriculture) endured by rejected applicants and so-called 'Dubliners' – the involuntarily repatriated refugees who return because they were fingerprinted in Italy:

These are very difficult people to be reinstated because it is a shock to be sent to Italy from, perhaps, Holland. In fact we called this place Maslah Square, in the name of a Somali boy who had been our guest in Via Cupa and then went to where his sister was and was then sent back here ... In Italy he committed suicide, he was put in a CAS in Pomezia and then he committed suicide and we decided to dedicate this square to him. Now we have had this specific case, but there are so many people who, once 'Dubliners', no longer find their place in Italy, and often on arrival at Fiumicino airport, sometimes they are not directed to the centres, so there are some who also stay on the street. They arrive in Fiumicino, 'Dubliners' from Holland go on the road, there is not even a reception presence and so now we have this kind of specificity (Barbara, Baobab).

Baobab Experience's mobile commons are therefore manifold. On the one hand, it is a solidarity response to the migrants who are outside the reception system, either because they never entered or because they have been expelled. For all of them, Baobab Experience provides shelter, food, healthcare services, legal assistance, schooling and counselling about job opportunities. On the other, it is a place supporting those migrants who aim to continue their journey once they have arrived in Europe without being trapped in the iron cage of the formal reception system. Baobab Experience's knowledge and networks can direct them migrants on the safest routes or provide them with shelter from hostile border management, resentment and xenophobia. All these functions constitute a form of contestation of migration policies through the repurposing and resignification of an unused car park into commons where solidarity practices respond to migrants' right to move freely. The string of evictions that Baobab Experience endured since its beginnings contributed significantly to repopulating Rome's informal settlements and slums, including the former factory known as 'Ex- Penicillina Leo'.

Ex-penicillina leo: missing commons

The former Penicillina Leo used to be the biggest pharmaceutical plant in Rome and one of the biggest in Europe. It was inaugurated in 1950 by the inventor of penicillin, Sir Alexander Fleming, and employed 1,600 people. The globalization and delocalisation of the late 1980s curtailed its revenues and profitability, until it was shut down in the early 2000s (LostItaly 2015). Following its closure, the building became the object of a legal controversy between the city council and the owner company, because of the abandonment of chemical waste in the area, which prevented the planned demolition and renovation of the area into an hotel complex. However, the industrial relic did not end up in the spotlight because of its toxicity for nearby inhabitants, but because of its abrupt re-population following the series of evictions carried out by the public authorities in the Tiburtina area from 2015, including that of the Baobab Experience. During summer 2018, the number of inhabitants at the former Penicillina Leo stood at 700. The site was eventually evicted on 10 December 2018 by hundreds of police in the presence of Minister of the Interior Matteo Salvini, while only few local activists and occupants protested outside. The small mobilisation was mainly due to the fact that the ex-Penicillina inhabitants did not develop resistance strategies or solidarity networks either among themselves or with grassroots urban movements (housing rights movements included), as they found the latter's demands unrelatable to their everyday experiences and necessities. Indeed, just as formations like BPM used to stress that housing squatters have re-appropriated their right to stay in the city through spatial and relational regeneration (Grazioli and Caciagli 2018), the emotional and physical wellbeing of the ex-Penicillina settlers was negatively affected by the poor environmental and infrastructural conditions in the factory. As explained by Saako, 26, a Gambian asylum seeker:

'I don't feel like a person anymore, living in there. You have no dignity, yet no other options. Making it through the day is simply overwhelming. Via Vannina wasn't good either, but the Penicillina is just like hell. Yet now I feel I don't have anywhere else to go'.

The sense of helplessness and de-humanisation experienced by S. also relates to the squatters' unfulfillment of their migratory projects, as their options were curtailed by the interplay of border policing, a lack of knowledge of the EU migratory regimes and, above all, a lack of connection and support in their transit and settlement – as the words of Mohammed, 28, an undocumented migrant from Nigeria, clearly demonstrate:

'I got in this place by chance. I arrived in Sicily, they gave me a train ticket to leave and I came to Rome. When I got to the Tiburtina station months ago I didn't have a place to stay, I didn't know any place in Rome and I didn't want to stop here, by the way. My plan was to go to France, maybe the UK, I speak English as my second language and I have a cousin there. I met a co-national of mine, he suggested I could crash in this place for a few days while I figured out where and how to go, and walked me in. I haven't left since. I don't know how to leave, I have no money. I feel very insecure outside but also inside. The police are often raiding the place and some guys got arrested, brought to the immigration centre, maybe deported, I am not sure. I am afraid to get caught but I don't want to stay here either. No one is really in control of what goes on in here'.

Mohammed's words show how the ex-Penicillina Leo represented a shelter and hideout for migrants in transit who did not have access to support networks on their way to Rome, but the combination of policing outside and seclusion inside ended up creating a 'trap' of segregation for those who did not find alternative arrangements. In addition, the illusion of temporariness and the fluid composition of the squatters (as a result of both autonomous mobility and forcible evictions) prevented them from forming a group that could attempt to consolidate community-building, everyday self-management and shared demands. Lastly, the endogenous and self-induced segregation of the inhabitants, coupled with the lack of internal organisation and trust among the squatters, prevented their mobilisation alongside and relations with grassroots urban movements, apart from NGOs providing first-aid and healthcare assistance. This was obvious during the December 2018 eviction, when the squatters did not enact any form of resistance or articulate their own demands together with the activists who were there in solidarity. Nevertheless, it is notable that the connection between the lack of internal organisation and increased vulnerability to repressive devices has been acknowledged by the evictees who managed to regroup in the area. They have decided to constitute themselves as an organised collective (Penicillina 2) to coordinate their legal defence against squatting charges, and to join housing rights movements' anti-eviction demonstrations.

Concluding remarks: different ways of commoning

Starting from a brief analysis of migration policy during the 'border regime crisis', this paper has investigated three housing struggles in Rome. Our purpose was to show how squatted areas can become urban commons and sites of contestation of migratory policies that aim to subjectivise migrants as people with little or no freedom of movement. From this perspective, the different types of self-made inhabitancy in Rome described in the previous sections respond primarily to migrants' demand for housing as an outcome of their spatial segregation and exploitation within the urban fabric. Furthermore, they configure an autonomous alternative to the institutional reception system. Lastly, they become emergency sites where migrants on the move can find shelter while planning their attempts to travel elsewhere.

Due to its daily organisational aspects, the 4 Stelle Occupato can be identified as an infrastructure of commoning. While housing and daily social reproduction are prioritised, these are supported by practices such as assembly-based decision-making, care of collective spaces and non-discriminatory ground rules coming from the housing rights movements' consolidated toolbox of practices. In addition, these organisational rites (Grazioli 2017, 2018) enable the squat's contentious politics within the political framework configured by housing rights movements. Lastly, the consolidation of the 4 Stelle Occupato as a radical infrastructure enables the squatters to mobilise the housing rights movements' contentious politics and practices to support their broader networks and communities in their mobility and settlement inside the city. Hence, the repurposing of the former EuroStar Congress into the housing squat 4 Stelle Occupato epitomises how squatting can become a multiplier of mobile as well as urban commons capable of contesting exploitative border regimes, and can unite grassroots urban movements and migrants' demands for dignified settlement and mobility.

The contestation of border regimes that restrict mobility was even clearer at Baobab Experience. The camp in Maslax Square used to be a *mobile* commons more invested in supporting migrants' autonomous mobility vis-à-vis the proliferation of bordering devices inside urban spaces, beyond cartographic borderlands. Unlike 4 Stelle Occupato which prioritises settlement, Baobab Experience aims at sheltering people who are either in transition to Europe or who are escaping the restrictive reception system which, operating according to the Dublin rules, would strand them in Italy. Hence, Baobab Experience's composition as well as its infrastructural arrangements are quite fluid. While it's composition is mainly of migrants transiting through Rome before moving to other countries, its infrastructural arrangements aim at empowering the 'world of knowledge, of information, of tricks for survival, of mutual care, of social relations, of services exchange, of solidarity and sociability' that Papadopoulos and

Tsianos (2013, 14) identify as mobile commons (see also Mezzadra and Neilson 2013). In contrast, these conditions were missing in the former Penicillina, where the isolation and limitations imposed by criminalising border and urban regimes were embodied in an informal settlement in which the squatters were deprived of the infrastructural, political and social materialities necessary for managing internal organising, community-building and political regrouping. This resulted in an eviction that was almost unopposed, with the majority of the squatters feeling that resistance was pointless for a place unworthy to stay and advocate for. Moreover, this experience of informal settlement did not empower migrants, but made them even more vulnerable to repression and detention. To conclude, the potentialities and contradictions highlighted by 4 Stelle Occupato, Baobab Experience and the former Penicillina show how self-made forms of inhabitancy can configure urban and mobile commons if they are structured as secure, liveable spatialities where migrants can forge reliable solidarity networks, create safe spaces of mutual care, and exert their autonomy and freedom of movement. As long as these conditions are maintained, they leave a legacy that can survive the uprooting of their physical location through repressive policing and evictions and contribute to the proliferation of further commons inside the city.

Notes

1. In this article we use the term 'migrant' interchangeably for 'economic migrant', 'undocumented migrant', 'asylum seeker' and 'refugee', unless one of these terms is required for more technical reasons and for the sake of clarity. By migrants we mean those persons who exercises their right to move to another country for better opportunities and living conditions. In this sense, there is no distinction between 'asylum seekers' and 'economic migrants', a distinction that has often been politicised and reified in order to classify and divide between 'deserving' and 'non-deserving', 'legal' and 'illegal' migrants.
2. 'Freedom of movement' usually refers to the specific right of EU citizens to move more or less freely across the EU along with goods, services and capital. However, we use this definition either to identify the 'secondary movement' to another EU country or the right to move within Italy without the geographical restrictions implied by being hosted in the reception system.
3. Available at http://fuoricampo.medicisenzafrontiere.it/Fuoricampo.pdf.
4. All the interviewees' names are replaced with pseudonyms.
5. Referring to the contracted company that managed the centre's services such as food and laundry until 2015.
6. This quote is an excerpt from a broader interview conducted in August 2018 during the eviction of the Sudanese centre at via Scorticabove, where the interviewee used to live prior to moving to 4 Stelle Occupato.

Disclosure statement

No potential conflict of interest was reported by the authors.

References

Aa. Vv. 2012. *Teatro Valle Occupato. La Rivolta Culturale Dei Beni*. Rome: Derive Approdi.

Armati, C. 2015. *La Scintilla. Dalla Valle Alla Metropoli, Una Storia Antagonista Della Lotta per La Casa*. Rome: Fandango Editore.

Bailey, S., and U. Mattei. 2013. "Social Movements as Constituent Power: The Italian Struggle for the Commons." *Indiana Journal of Global Legal Studies* 20 (2): 965–1013. doi:10.2979/indjglolegstu.20.2.965.

Bianchi, I. 2018. "The Post-Political Meaning of the Concept of Commons: The Regulation of the Urban Commons in Bologna." *Space and Polity* 22 (3): 287–306. doi:10.1080/13562576.2018.1505492.

Blitz, B., A. d'Angelo, E. Kofman, and N. Montagna. 2017. "Health Challenges in Refugee Reception: Dateline Europe." *International Journal of Environmental Research and Public Health* 14 (12): 1484. doi:10.3390/ijerph14121484.

Bollier, D. 2015. *La Rinascita Dei Commons*. Viterbo: Stampa Alternativa.

Borri, G. 2017. "Humanitarian Protraction Status. The Production of (Im)Mobile Subjects between Turin and Berlin." *Etnografia E Ricerca Qualitativa* X (1): 55–74.

Bresnihan, P., and M. Byrne. 2014. "Escape into the City: Everyday Practices of Commoning and the Production of Urban Space in Dublin." *Antipode* 47 (1): 36–54. doi:10.1111/anti.12105.

Carrozza, C., and E. Fantini. 2016. "The Italian Water Movement and the Politics of the Commons." *Water Alternatives* 9 (1): 99–119.

Cellamare, C. 2014. "The Self-Made City." In *Global Rome. Changing Faces of the Eternal City*, edited by I. Clough Marinaro and B. Thomassen, 205–218. Bloomington, In Indiana University Press.

Centro sociale Askatasuna. 2013. *A Sarà Düra! Storie Di Vita E Di Militanza No Tav*. Rome: Derive Approdi.

Conlon, D. 2011. "Waiting: Feminist Perspectives on the Spacings/Timings of Migrant (Im) Mobility." *Gender, Place & Culture* 18:3: 353–360. doi:10.1080/0966369X.2011.566320.

Davoli, C. 2019. "Le Occupazioni Abitative a Roma: Una "Pratica Di Movimento" per Il Diritto All'abitare." In *Roma in Transizione. Governo, Strategie, Metabolismi E Quadri Di Vita Di Una Metropoli*, edited by A. Coppola and G. Punziano, 305–314. 2nd ed. Rome-Milan: Planum Publisher.

De Angelis, M. 2017. *Omnia Sunt Communia. On the Commons and the Transformation to Postcapitalism*. London: Zed Books.

De Angelis, R. 1991. *Gli Erranti. Nuove Povertà E Immigrazione Nella Metropoli*. Rome: Edizioni Kappa.

De Genova, N., ed. 2017. *The Borders of "Europe": Autonomy of Migration, Tactics of Bordering*. Durham, NC: Duke University Press.

Fontanari, E., and M. Ambrosini. 2018. "Into the Interstices: Everyday Practices of Refugees and Their Supporters in Europe's Migration 'Crisis'." *Sociology* 52 (3): 587–603. doi:10.1177/0038038518759458.

Frontiere, M. S. 2016. "Fuoricampo. Richiedenti Asilo E Rifugiati in Italia: Insediamenti Informali E Marginalità Sociale." Accessed: https://www.abuondiritto.it/it/privazione-della-libert%c3%a0/studi-e-ricerche/1939-uscire-dal-ghetto.html

Gentili, M., and J. Hoekstra. 2018. "Houses without People and People without Houses: A Cultural and Institutional Exploration of an Italian Paradox." *Housing Studies* 34 (3): 1–23.

Grazioli, M. 2017. "From Citizens to Citadins: Rethinking Right to the City inside Housing Squats in Rome, Italy." *Citizenship Studies* 21 (4): 393–408. doi:10.1080/13621025.2017.1307607.

Grazioli, M. 2018. "The 'Right to the City' in the Post-Welfare Metropolis. Community-Building, Autonomous Infrastructures and Urban Commons in Rome's Self-Organised Housing Squats." PhD Thesis: University of Leicester.

Grazioli, M., and C. Caciagli. 2018. "Resisting the Neoliberal Urban Fabric: Housing Rights Movements and the Re-Appropriation of the 'Right to the City' in Rome, Italy." *Voluntas* 1 (Social Movements): 1–15.

Hardin, G. 1968. "The Tragedy of the Commons." *Science* 162: 1243–1248.

Hodkinson, S. 2012. "The New Urban Enclosures." *City* 16 (5): 500–518. doi:10.1080/13604813.2012.709403.

La Repubblica. 2018a. "Irreperibili 50 Migranti Della Nave Diciotti. Si Sono Allontanati Dal Centro Di Rocca Di Papa". *La Repubblica*, Accessed 5 September 2018.

Lazio, R. "Piano Straordinario Emergenza Abitativa Nel Lazio.", http://www.regione.lazio.it/rl_urp/?vw=newsdettaglio&id=374

Linebaugh, P. 2008. *The Magna Carta Manifesto: Liberties and Commons for All*. Berkeley: University of California Press.

LostItaly. 2015. "Leo Farmaceutica." Accessed 11 Oct 2018. https://www.lostitaly.it/site/leo-farmaceutica

Mattei, U. 2011. "Institutionalizing the Commons: An Italian Primer. PART I.: Political Background. Indignados Italian Style". Accessed: https://commonsblog.files.wordpress.com/2007/10/mattei-italian-commons-chapter-short.pdf

Mattei, U. 2012. *Beni Comuni. Un Manifesto*. Bari: Laterza.

Mezzadra, S., and B. Neilson. 2013. *Border as Method, Or, the Multiplication of Labor*. Durham, NC: Duke University Press.

Micciarelli, G. 2017. "Introduzione All'uso Civico E Collettivo Urbano. La Gestione Diretta Dei Beni Comuni Urbani." *Munus* 1: 135–162.

Montagna, N. 2006. "The Decommodification of Urban Space and the *Centro Sociale Rivolta*." *City: Analysis of Urban Trends, Culture, Theory, Policy, Action* 10 (3): 295–304. doi:10.1080/13604810600980663.

MSF. 2016. *Fuoricampo. Richiedenti Asilo e Rifugiati in Italia: Insediamenti Informali e Marginalità Sociale*.

Mudu, P. 2006. "Patterns of Segregation in Contemporary Rome." *Urban Geography* 27 (5): 422–440. doi:10.2747/0272-3638.27.5.422.

Mudu, P. 2014. "Ogni Sfratto Sarà Una Barricata: Squatting for Housing and Social Conflct in Rome." In *Squatters' Movement in Europe: Commons and Autonomy as Alternatives to Capitalism*, 136–163. Squatting Europe Kollective ed. London: Pluto Press.

Nur, N., and A. Sethman. 2017. "Migration and Mobilization for the Right to Housing in Rome. New Urban Frontiers?" In *Migration, Squatting and Radical Autonomy: Resistance and Destabilization*, edited by P. Mudu and S. Chattopadhyay, 78–92. London: Routledge.

Ostrom, E. 1990. *Governing the Commons: The Evolution of Institutions for Collective Action*. Cambridge, UK: Cambridge University Press.

Palermo, P., and V. Muscella. 2014. "4stellehotel.it An Ordinary Day in an Extra Ordinary Place." Accessed 19 Jun 2019. 19/06,2019. http://www.4stellehotel.it/.

Papadopoulos, D. 2018. *Experimental Politics. Technoscience, Alterontologies and More than Social Movements*. Durham. NC: Duke University Press.

Papadopoulos, D., and V. Tsianos. 2013. "After Citizenship: Autonomy of Migration, Organisational Ontology and Mobile Commons." *Citizenship Studies* 17 (2): 178–196. doi:10.1080/13621025.2013.780736.

Picozza, F. 2017. "Dubliners Unthinking Displacement, Illegality, and Refugeeness within Europes Geographies of Asylum." In *The Borders of "Europe": Autonomy of Migration, Tactics of Bordering*, edited by N. De Genova, 233–254. Durham, NC: Duke University Press.

Pinelli, B. 2016. "Politiche, Persone, Immagini." In *Dopo L'approdo. Un Racconto per Immagini E Parole Sui Richiedenti Asilo in Italia*, edited by B. Pinelli and L. Ciabarri, 49–86. Milan: Edit Press.

Pinelli, B. 2017. "Borders, Politics and Subjects. Introductory Notes on Refugee Research in Europe." *Etnografia E Ricerca Qualitativa* X (1): 5–24.

Pruijt, H. 2013. "The Logic of Urban Squatting." *International Journal of Urban and Regional Research* 37 (1): 19–45. doi:10.1111/ijur.2013.37.issue-1.

Repubblica, L. 2018b. "Roma, 57mila Persone Famiglie Sono in Emergenza Abitativa." Accessed 22 Nov 2018. https://roma.repubblica.it/cronaca/2018/11/19/news/roma_l_allarme_dei_cost ruttori_a_roma_57_mila_famiglie_sono_in_emergenza_abitativa_-212056587

S.M.U.R. 2014. *Roma Città Autoprodotta. Ricerca Urbana E Linguaggi Artistici*. Self Made Urbanism Rome ed. Roma: Manifestolibri.

Squatting Europe Kollective. 2014. *The Squatters' Movement in Europe. Commons and Autonomy as Alternatives to Capitalism*. London: Pluto Press.

Subirats, J. 2012. "The Commons: Beyond the Market Vs. State Dilemma". *Opendemocracy*, accessed 17 Jan 2019. https://www.opendemocracy.net/joan-subirats/commons-beyond-market-vs-state-dilemma

Tazzioli, M. 2014. *Spaces of Governmentality: Autonomous Migration and the Arab Uprisings*. London: Rowman & Littlefield.

Yuval Davis, N., G. Wemyss, and K. Cassidy. 2018. "Everyday Bordering, Belonging and the Reorientation of British Immigration Legislation." *Sociology* 52 (2): 228–244. doi:10.1177/0038038517702599.

The micropolitics of border struggles: migrants' squats and inhabitance as alternatives to citizenship

Deanna Dadusc

ABSTRACT

This paper discusses the struggles of the We Are Here movement in Amsterdam as resistance to both securitarian and humanitarian border regimes. It explores the tensions between everyday forms of commoning emerging in migrants' squats and technologies of enclosure and capture. In the first place, the paper contends that the creation of housing squats marked an important shift in migrants' struggles that went from acts of protest to the performance of resistance at the level of the micropolitics of borders. By squatting buildings and creating common living spaces, current struggles mobilize material, affective and political solidarities and constitute a politics of inhabitance beyond and against dependency on the state and humanitarian practices. The second part of the paper discusses the government's attempts to repress, govern and enclose the We Are Here movement within confined fields of action. With negotiations and humanitarian concessions through the provision of emergency shelters, local authorities attempted to re-direct the movement into politics of rights and recognitions. However, these tactics did not succeed to contain the struggle in its entirety: many migrants rejected humanitarian solutions, continued to create radical home spaces through squatting, enacting a politics of inhabitance beyond citizenship.

Introduction

Beginning in 2012, in the Netherlands, isolated acts of migrants' protest have begun to consolidate into long-term collective mobilizations with the creation of the We Are Here movement. We Are Here is a movement composed of migrants whose requests for asylum have been rejected but who often cannot legally be deported to their countries of origin because the Dutch government considers them unsafe. Yet, they have been ordered to leave the Netherlands and are therefore stranded in a legal limbo that denies access to basic needs including housing, health care, employment and education. As an alternative to living on the streets, or to being monitored and isolated in state-run asylum centres, while waiting for a policy change or regularization of their status, 'We Are Here' participants decided to break-open these circuits of invisibility and oppression. They began squatting large vacant buildings and creating common spaces for shelter, for collective mobilization against the border regime, as well as for the organization of alternative forms of life and social relations.

Despite tensions, conflict and constant precarity, the inhabitants of these spaces exit and subvert the material forms of isolation and dependency, as well as the affective politics of fear and silence.

In line with other contributions to this special issue, this paper establishes a differentiation between the provision of housing through emergency and humanitarian shelters, and the practice of home-making though squatting (Dadusc et al. this issue). Drawing on critical humanitarian studies (Agier 2011; Fassin 2011; Weizman 2011; Ticktin 2016), the paper argues that the practice of squatting constitutes a practice of resistance not only to the criminalization of migration but also to humanitarian forms of government operating through care/control principles. In contrast to humanitarian and state-run shelters, squatting becomes a practice of commoning against the enclosures of the border regimes with the creation of common spaces and solidarities constituting a resistance to the violence, isolation and segregation of both securitarian and humanitarian enclosures (for a broader discussion of these forms of commoning see Dadusc et al. 2019 and De Angelis 2019).

The formation of political subjects and their interrelation with the norms of citizenship (either from above or from below, recognized or performed) cannot be disentangled from forms of governance, control and capture by the state (Rigby and Schlembach 2013). Following Asli Ikizoglu Erensu's (2016) call for the need to rethink the relation between citizenship and political subjectivity, this paper argues that, despite making claims for integration based on citizenship, the We Are Here movement performs resistance to the micropolitics of borders, as these struggles are enacted and embodied in each aspect of people's lives, subjectivities and affective relations. The everyday forms of commoning emerging in migrants' squats entail the creation of modes of existence that are not defined by formal or informal citizenship, documentation and government-granted human rights.

Drawing on the definition of *inhabitance* as an alternative to citizenship proposed in the introduction to this special issue (Dadusc, Grazioli, and Martinez 2019), this paper highlights the micro-political, affective and ambivalent dimension of resistance that defy both humanitarian borders and the codes of conduct accompanying the performance of citizenship. Through the We Are Here struggle, *inhabitance* constitutes a radical practice of occupying space, of home-making beyond and against both the normative and informal codes of citizenship, as well as their disciplining implications. Inhabitance is not just a desire or a longing for recognition, but the affirmation of presence, a here-and-now praxis of existence: it entails an active re-appropriation of time, space and social relations, despite attempts to confine people in a limbo of semi-existence. Moreover, the formulation of a politics of inhabitance, rather than of citizenship, provides the grounds for new forms of solidarity that dismantle existing host-guest hierarchies between those who hold citizenship and those who desire citizenship, otherwise addressed as *subjects of lack*.

After outlining the micropolitics of the We Are Here struggle for inhabitance, the second part of the paper discusses the government's reaction. Particular attention is given to the role of humanitarian discourses and practices, and to the ambivalences and tensions that emerged in this context. Indeed, the language of humanitarian emergency and the technologies of tolerance and negotiations employed by local authorities aimed at channeling the We Are Here movement within a confined field of action: namely, turning spaces of *contention* into spaces of *containment*, by fixing ungovernable practices into a static mode, re-establishing forms of dependency to the state and pushing the formulation the movement agendas in the language of rights and recognitions.

The micropolitics of border regimes: the security-humanitarian nexus

European borders are increasingly externalized through a variety of agreements, negotiations and militarization (Bigo 2014), while internal borders are becoming multiplied, diffuse and ubiquitous (Balibar 2009; Vaughan-Williams 2008; Rygiel 2011). An increasing variety of institutions act as formal and informal border control agents: these include landlords, health services providers, labour agencies, schools (Salter 2006; Anderson, Sharma, and Wright 2009; Jones and Johnson 2016). In the Netherlands, during the past decades, undocumented migrants have increasingly been subject to stricter surveillance and security measures (Broeders 2010; Van der Woude, van der Leun, and Nijland 2014) through what Stumpf (2006) calls 'crimmigration': namely, the increased convergence of criminal laws and migration laws. Moreover, techniques of repression go beyond the legalistic elements of criminalization, as they extend to the illegalization of every aspect of racialized bodies and lives, creating hostile environments for migration (Aas 2011) and placing the border in migrants' everyday life (Jones and Johnson 2016). This production of illegality in everyday lives (De Genova 2002) configures as an interrelation of coercion over migrants bodies, governing their affects and subjectivities.

Two legal measures were responsible for the implementation of crimmigration in the Netherlands, which on the one hand contributed to an overall hostile environment to migration, and on the other centralized the provision of services for undocumented migrants, including housing, in the hands of state-run agencies. In the 1990s, the *Koppelingswet* (Linkage Act), in line with the European pattern of the 1990s, limited access to social services such as education and health care, as well as the possibility to work legally (see Van der Leun 2006; Van der Leun and Kloosterman 2006). Together with stricter monitoring and registration techniques, between 1999 and 2007 the capacity of administrative detention was increased from 1000 to 4000 units (Leerkes and Broeders 2010, 835).

In 2007, the *Vremdelingenwet 2007* (Aliens Act 2007)[1] placed new restrictions on undocumented migrants and asylum-seekers and centralized authority and responsibility in the hands of the Immigration and Naturalization Agency (IND) and of the Repatriation Agency (DT&V). As a consequence, municipalities and local organizations were not allowed to provide assistance and support to illegalized migrants, and existing emergency shelters were replaced with state-run facilities. With the 2010 Law on Identification and the Benefit Entitlement Act, the Dutch government extended the technologies of criminalization even further. Since then, and through the enforcement of the so-called Return Directive, rejected asylum seekers are handed a notification to leave the Netherlands within 48 h, and are banned from re-entering Dutch territory. Non-departure is considered a criminal offence punishable with detention and deportation (Tweede Kamer der Staten-Generaal 2013, 1). Those who cannot leave are then directed toward an asylum centre in Ter Apel, where they may stay for a maximum of 12 weeks.

The government mobilized nationalist discourses to give legitimacy to these legislations, framing them as necessary steps to protect social services for nationals, to guarantee social and cultural cohesion, and to lower crime rates (Leerkes, Engbersen, and Van der Leun 2012). Moreover, these laws went hand in hand with a redefinition of residence rights and with new moral discourses around the illegality of residence. According to the Dutch cabinet, Dutch residence is determined not simply by someone's presence in the country, but by their capacity to integrate culturally, and to respect norms and values of Dutch society, namely to perform good citizenship:

> Education, speaking the language, and being economically independent are the foundations for the best possible integration. The ones who fulfill these demands and who contribute to our society are, and will be welcome. Illegal residence does not fit in such a society. Illegal aliens [sic] do not fully participate in our society [...]. Further, illegal residence goes hand in hand with many forms of nuisance and criminality[2]. (Tweede Kamer der Staten-Generaal 2013, 1)

While this ignores the fact that illegality is not an ontological condition, but is instead defined and produced by the State itself, it also poses Dutch identity, norms and values as intrinsically superior.[3] Accordingly, not only citizenship but also residence on the Dutch territory is framed as a privilege to be granted on the basis of people's capacity to conform to Dutch norms, values and culture. This resonates with Étienne Balibar's (2016) reflections on how the production of the figure of the so-called 'illegal migrant' as a 'foreign body' has become the major site for the production of codes of citizenship and to the 'citizen's body'.

As it will be discussed in relation to the We Are Here movement, humanitarian modes of governance of migrants' bodies, lives and voices increasingly complement state criminalization and securitization (Pallister-Wilkins 2015; Ticktin 2016; Cuttitta 2018). Humanitarian borders (Walters 2010) are enforced by addressing migrants as a humanitarian emergency, victimizing them as vulnerable objects of lack and of need, and mobilizing allegedly 'a-political' ideals of universality and benevolence (Hyndman 2000; Nyers 2013; Vaughan-Williams 2015). Instead of manifesting themselves through direct forms of repression, humanitarian borders are coercive, disciplinary and biopolitical modes of power, governing and controlling by fostering life as well as through technologies of care that are strictly entangled with control over migrants bodies and lives (Fassin 2011; Ticktin 2016). Rather than providing an alternative to illegalization and criminalization, humanitarian interventions co-produce and fortify multiple forms of sovereign control (Pallister-Wilkins 2018). As much as securitarian approaches, they keep migrants in a 'state of emergency' and in relations of dependency which trap them in a condition of spatial and temporal immobility (Tazzioli 2014). Therefore, humanitarian assistance and protection constitute security devices that operate alongside, and not outside of, the violence of borders.

The combination of these technologies creates complex forms of enclosure that go beyond detention of individuals, forced mobility or forced immobility within certain territories. Enclosures manifest in a multiplicity of technologies for the intervention on migrants' bodies and everyday lives, from spatial segregation (spatial enclosures), suspension in temporal limbos (temporal enclosures), dependency on care-control practices (humanitarian enclosures) as well as labels and discourses that legitimize structural harms and that divert the attention from the violence of borders (epistemic enclosure). Moreover, as argued below, these technologies also constitute *affective enclosures*, through intervening on migrants' capacity to exist and to resist by keeping them in a condition of fear, invisibility, precarity, silence and dependency.

Affective enclosures

Since the emergence of the so-called 'affective turn' (Clough and Halley 2007; Gregg and Seigworth 2010), feminist, queer and postcolonial scholars have attempted to subvert dichotomous understandings of political action, developing concepts that would highlight complex inter-relations between ethics and politics (Bargetz 2015). These approaches aim at understanding the political dynamics and potential of affects as political and cultural technologies of power, implying not only normative but alsoaffective modes of government (Bargetz 2015; Boler 2004; Clough 2010; Pedwell 2012). Indeed, the spheres of everyday life of affects and subject formations cannot be separated from politics as these are in themselves objects of government (Revel 2009). The affective technologies of power circulating through border regimes constitute forms of subjection 'through the material production of specific modes of experience' (D'Aoust 2014, 269) to create a *micropolitics* of borders: micropolitics is here intended as the level where politics and ethics intersect, where affects, social relations and everyday lives cannot be separated from what are generally defined as political technologies of government (Read 2003).

Fortier's (2016) understanding of *affective* citizenship provides a key tool for understanding the role of affects in constituting citizenship and state/citizen relations, as well as for addressing the affective technologies of enclosure that are mobilized through humanitarian practices and discourses. Indeed, citizenship is not only bound with government or corporate disciplinary power relations but entails the political mobilization of affects, which constrain, define and demarcate populations (ibid): namely, governing technologies which define legitimate modalities of how to feel as citizens, how to protest as citizens, how to claim rights as citizens, amongst others.

As affects are tools of power, they are also important sites of resistance (Butler 1997; Ahmed 2008; Hynes 2013; Pedwell and Whitehead 2012). Moreover, if what characterizes the *micropolitics* of borders is the governmental power to manage populations not only through rights and forms of inclusions/exclusion, but through the *conduct of conduct*[4] (Foucault 2007), namely the production of specific affects, values, desires and modes of life (Cadman 2010; Lazzarato 2009; Read 2003), then practices of resistance reconfigure themselves as attempts to create different modes of thinking, acting and of relating to the norms and rules that govern lives. According to Fortier *affective citizenship* can thus become 'a site for radical modes of belonging that might be shaped by governing technologies but one that also refuses to be determined by it (Fortier 2016, 1039).

Enclosures and subjection, indeed, do not come without resistance. As argued in the following section, as much as criminalization, victimization and the violence of borders become diffuse and ubiquitous, so do migrants' struggles (Ataç, Rygiel, and Stierl 2016; Stierl 2018). While modes of governance and enclosures seek to produce, channel and contain spaces of possibility (of mobility, action and existence), these are constantly disrupted by a multiplicity of acts of subversion that counter, escape and create cracks in the smooth operation of bordering regimes (Mezzadra 2015). Whereas many forms of contestation are moved against the securitarian management of migration, there are limited (political and academic) discussions about the need to resist humanitarian enclosures and their affective technologies of governance that come with citizenship.

The micropolitics of border struggles: we are here to stay

In the Netherlands, as in other European cities (see contributions to this special issue as well as Mudu and Chattopadhyay 2017), squatting has been a tool of undocumented migrants to mobilize protest and to create platforms for mobilization against the bordering of Europe, as well as to open common spaces for organizing their lives and for taking their needs into their own hands. Since that winter of 2012, 'We Are Here' squatted about 50 buildings, including a former church, office spaces, former schools, and vacant residential premises. These squatted buildings are used for shelter as well as for creating social and political hubs where different groups of people can act in solidarity, mobilize protest and organize themselves collectively and autonomously.

The creation of housing squats as opposed to the containment in asylum centres or camps marks an important shift in migrants' struggles and anti-state practices. The peculiarity of migrants' squats is the refusal to reproduce humanitarian affective politics of dependency, in favour of modes of organization based on solidarity between documented and undocumented activists and squatters. While the security-humanitarian nexus strand people in a spatio-temporal limbo of uncertainty (Hyndman and Giles 2011) and dependency, by organizing collectively, protesting on the streets and creating common homes, the We Are Here movement challenges the affective politics that keep them 'stuck in the present' (Brun 2016), and exercise what Catherine Brun defined as 'agency-in-waiting' (Brun 2015), prefiguring the possibility of alternative spatio-temporal, political and affective relations. The networks of solidarity by local activists that emerged around squatted spaces do not merely seek to help migrants survive – they create places where a livable existence and everyday resistance go hand-in-hand. Rather than being passive receivers of help and subject to care-control practices, the inhabitants of these spaces live collectively, organize daily activities, including collective cooking, workshops, discussions and demonstrations to raise awareness and to build connections with allies and supporters.

The constitution of solidarity networks between local squatters and We Are Here, led to the mobilisation of common struggles that exceed the walls of each squat, and that enable the formation of common *political* subjectivities which do not take citizenship as a referent. While groups of local squatters have initially supported We Are Here with the technical skills required to open new spaces, We Are Here activists have often contributed to, and participated in, a variety of political spaces and mobilizations organized by local squatters. Hierarchies between documented and undocumented people are here challenged by creating modalities of *mutual* solidarity and the formulation of common struggles that disrupt *host-guest* relations imposed by the codes of citizenship (Squire and Darling 2013). Solidarity is here expressed as a political practice rather than a humanitarian approach, an act of resistance rather than an act of assistance.

Therefore, the struggles of the We Are Here movement go beyond right claiming and recognition and constitute semi-permanent infrastructures for mobile commons (Papadopoulos and Tsianos 2013) to circulate, to sediment and to multiply. The occupation of squatted homes brings border struggles to the intimate level of homes, as spaces to create the possibilities for different social, political and affective relations based on solidarity, cooperation and mutual aid. The goal is not to provide plasters that make the situation more tolerable, nor to ameliorate the conditions of oppression, but to transform the very foundations of racialized border regimes, as to counter the operation of the military-humanitarian borders nexus.

Besides the formation of new *political* subjectivities that do not take citizenship as a referent, these struggles perform resistance in the field of affect and *ethics*: silenced individuals, who needed to hide and wait in a condition of constant fear and dependency, became active and powerful collectives, appropriating and inhabiting urban, social and political spaces, creating collective platforms to challenge the affective technologies of border regimes and of the codes of conduct of citizenship.

Inhabitance is here proposed to address the commoning *praxis* in migrants' squats, namely the permanent constitution of common struggles, spaces and networks of solidarity, which despite the precarity of each squat, are not temporary ruptures. Moreover, inhabitance entails a radical *ethics*, as it brings the struggle to everyday forms of social reproduction, to the constitution of spaces for radical affects, subjectivities and social relations (Revel 2009) that border regimes seek to enclose, displace and erase. Moreover, inhabitance figures as a *politics* of transformation of the codes that define citizenship. While citizenship sets political practices within a fixed and governable field, in these autonomous spaces there is an attempt to make new webs of relation possible. By *inhabiting* common living spaces, current struggles mobilize material, affective and political forms of solidarity that engender resistance to spatial and social injustice, but also constitute grassroots forms of organization beyond and against the state, challenging the operation of borders, and the way migrants bodies and affects are disciplined and governed. Inhabitance as a politics, an ethics and a *praxis*, can entail the constitution of living alternatives to the violence of borders, creating relational webs and bridges in the face of enclosures.

Yet, there is always a tension between these liberatory practices and technologies of enclosure and capture (Papadopoulos, Stephenson, and Tsianos 2008). The following section discusses the government's attempts to repress, govern and enclose them within a confined field of action. As the eviction of each squat lead to the opening of new ones, direct forms of repression through criminalization were replaced by more subtle modes of governance, in an attempt to intervene on the We Are Here's capacity to create ungovernable struggles. Here, a key question emerges: to what extent is it possible to produce forms of resistance to the process of subject-making based on humanitarian principles, as well as to the *conduct of conduct* that comes with the requirement of performing good citizenship by those who are excluded from citizenship?

From spaces of contention to spaces of containment

Despite squatting in the Netherlands having been criminalized in 2010 (see Dadusc 2019), local authorities reacted to 'We Are Here' squats by refusing to enforce the law, and instead undertook an approach that favoured tolerance and negotiation. Local authorities argued that the We are Here squats were to be treated differently than other squats because of the 'humanitarian nature' of the movement. Yet, rather than ameliorating the conditions of migrants, these strategies resulted in stricter monitoring and control. The We Are Here squats were tolerated in an attempt to depoliticize and silence the struggle and to avoid the formulation of structural change to the border regimes. Granting residence permits to key figures of the group and providing emergency shelters to parts of the group was used as a strategy to break down existing solidarities and create internal tensions and differentiations.

After the occupation of the first building, the *Vluchtkerk*, the Mayor demanded a list of names of the migrants involved in the movement. At the end of the same year, after several occupations and evictions, We Are Here squatted an empty office building in front of the *Rijks Museum*: literally, the museum of the Empire, which uncritically celebrates the Dutch Golden Age and colonial violence. This direct action made 'We Are Here' visible, placing migrants presence at the centre, rather than at the margins of the colonial Empire that created the conditions for the so-called 'refugee crisis' to emerge in the first place. This occupation aimed at dismantling the dialectic between margin and centre, between citizens who belong to the city and the undesirables presences excluded from political and social space (Squire 2016).

As a forced eviction would have provoked undesired visible protests, the Mayor opted to negotiate and offered a temporary emergency shelter in a former prison (*Havenstraat*). Access to the shelter/prison was granted under the condition that the hosted migrants would cooperate with immigration in the assessment of their cases and with their return to their home country: namely, their own deportation. Most members of the movement were about to refuse the offer, as accommodation in a former prison – with former prison guards, curfews, controlled access and strict monitoring of daily activities – was not considered a safe option. However, threatened with immediate eviction, the group accepted the offer and voluntarily left the squat. Only once all inhabitants of the squat signed the agreement, the Mayor announced that only those on the pre-existing list were allowed to access the shelter/prison, thereby dividing the group and leaving homeless those who were not registered (Dadusc 2016).

A few weeks later the excluded part of the group squatted a municipality-owned building in Amsterdam-Bijlmer: the *Vluchtgarage*. The building lacked running water and electricity, and was situated next to a mosque. Bijlmer is a neighbourhood at the edge of the city, built in the 1980s to host the post-colonial diaspora of migrant workers. It is often referred to as a *ghetto*, due to the spatial segregation of ethnic minorities. While most of the squatted spaces in the city centre were evicted within a few weeks, here the group was allowed to stay for 18 months. However, the local council refused to provide access to water and electricity, leaving the building in precarity and unfit for human habitation.

In April 2014, after a few months in this situation of spatial segregation, a part of the group decided to leave the *Vluchtgarage* and to bring the struggle back to the city centre, squatting four buildings in a gentrifying neighbourhood (*Ten Katestraat – Amsterdam Oud West*). Three former social housing buildings and a warehouse, all in the process of demolition, were renovated by the inhabitants to create living spaces and a social centre: the *Vluchtmarkt*. Here several workshops and demonstrations were organized, including the international 'March for Freedom'[5] (see Nigg 2015), which connected We Are Here to broader international struggles for the freedom of movement and against Frontex.

While in previous cases, the evictions of the 'We Are Here' group were approached differently to other (criminalized) squats, in the case of *Vluchtmarkt*, the public prosecutor, the chief of the police and the Mayor decided to enforce the existing law that criminalizes squatting and evicted all the buildings. According to the public prosecutor, in this case, a different approach was legitimized because, while other We Are Here squats served as humanitarian shelters, the *Vluchtmarkt* constituted a political space. As he stated during a conversation with the lawyer of the group: 'these are not refugees, they are no-border squatters'. A clear differentiation was made between, on the one hand, squats like the

Vluchtgarage, operating as emergency shelters and as 'spaces of containment' which could be tolerated and on the other, 'spaces of contention' which kept the struggle alive and therefore had to be repressed. Therefore, tolerance of some squats operated as a mechanism to leave power relations undisturbed (Brown 2009) and as a tool of governmentality to de-politicize and pacify the We Are Here struggles. This was achieved by setting the boundaries, establishing the limits and the norms of what could be done (and how) in order to comply with specific conditions of acceptability, while maintaining the threat of repression (Dadusc 2019).

Bed, bread and bath: humanitarian enclosures

In parallel to these events, in January 2013, the Dutch Homeless Organization and the Protestant Church, in collaboration with the Conference of European Churches (CEC) submitted a complaint to the European Committee of Social Rights (ECSR).[6] The CEC demanded that the Dutch government should take *basic* social rights seriously, and provide shelter and food for everyone regardless of their legal status. Non-provision of minimal social services to the undocumented was addressed as an offence against article 25 of the Human Rights Declaration. In response, the ECSR issued an 'immediate measure' to the Dutch authorities, inviting them 'to suspend the operation of the Linkage Act with regard to shelter, food and clothing, so as to prevent further harm and safeguard health and life.

In 2014 after the recommendations by the ECSR and subsequent pressure from humanitarian organizations, municipalities implemented the so-called 'Bed, Bath and Bread' policy (BBB) to provide emergency night-shelter for rejected asylum seekers. This resulted in tensions between central and local governments, with the former refusing to provide assistance to illegalized migrants, and the latter attempting to implement humanitarian solutions. The provision of shelter and food was presented by a number of municipalities as a solution to an alleged humanitarian emergency and as a measure that would allow the Netherlands to comply with human rights laws (Starling 2015).

This could be considered a political victory, a recognition of undocumented migrants' *right to rights*, and the successful outcomes of We Are Here demands and protests. After the implementation of the BBB, part of the group accepted the conditions and moved to the night shelters. Yet, as a response to the 'Bed, Bath and Bread' policy (BBB), the We Are Here movement also organized several demonstrations and re-defined BBB as 'Blah Blah Blah'. Instead of accepting humanitarian emergency shelters, a part of the group rejected the fulfilment of their basic human rights and the confinement of their struggles within these frameworks and refused the choice as offered. As stated in an open letter to the Amsterdam Municipality in response to the BBB plan:

> We have a lot of questions about the concept of 'night shelters', because it means that you will be on the street again every morning (...) For migrants it means that they are punished every day for their request for help and that night care leads to being displaced, without any prospect of a solution (...). For migrants, only a sleeping place is no progress compared to the situation they are currently in. We prefer to stay in a leaky and cold *Vluchtgarage*, than to be driven into the streets during the day.[7]

Moreover, as a result of the implementation of the BBB, the Municipality argued that housing squats were not a necessity anymore, as basic human rights had been granted and shelter had been provided. This created a divide between those who challenged the politics of borders through illegalized and undesirable forms of action (i.e. squatting houses, direct action, refusing 'human rights' based solutions, rejecting night-shelters) and those who, often advised by humanitarian organizations, or afraid of turning the state against themselves and of jeopardizing their asylum applications, diverted from these possibilities of mobilization. Those who refused to be accommodated in emergency shelters and who currently continue to squat are being delegitimized, considered ungrateful, and further criminalized by means of eviction and repression, rather than negotiation. On the other hand, 'humanitarian solutions' towards We Are Here were granted at the price of cooperation with the authorities, providing support only to those migrants who wished to register their presence, to make their irregular status visible to the authorities and to cooperate with their own deportation.

Humanitarian 'remedies' such as the provision of BBB shelter and containment in the former prison were not only offered at the cost of higher monitoring and control but operated as a strategy to divide, discipline and tame ungovernable forms of action, thereby co-producing, rather than challenging, existing forms of enclosure. As in the cases outlined above, tolerance and humanitarian forms of intervention are inscribed in a relationship of power between benevolent donor and receiver (Fassin 2011; Ticktin 2016), and came with conditions and a political cost. Historically, the 'Dutch' model of regulated tolerance and compromise aimed at reducing the possibilities for unexpected events, conditioning the circumstances and the conditions under which things happen. *Gedogen*, the Dutch word for the 'regulated tolerance' refers to the mode of negotiation between the government and other social actors, aimed at reaching agreements rather than conflict (Brants 1998; Buruma 2007). Through negotiations and constant dialogue the desired effect of keeping potential 'dangers' close to the government gaze, rather than in opposition to it, thereby exercising forms of control to tame, rather than simply suppress, subversive forces. However, the boundaries between tolerable and unaccep-table modes of action can be extended or reduced at any time.

Similar to the negotiations and tolerance of certain squats, humanitarian shelters operated as a technology of government to contain and channel migrants' struggles within limited fields of acceptability; differentiating between legitimate and illegitimate demands and delineating the codes of conduct of good citizenship for people without citizenship. The promise of rights and forms of humanitarian assistance are often operating as smoke and mirrors; honey traps that confine the possibility for thinking and acting beyond the fields of possibility defined by the state. Those who are excluded from formal access to rights, or from the possibility of claiming rights, are still expected to formulate demands and claim recognition in the field of institutional politics and in dialogue with the state. These expectations produce disciplined subjects that express their struggles within govern-able channels, that seek recognition from the state and that as such are forced to comply with the norms and laws of the state that exclude them.

In this context, waiting for recognition, seeking citizenship and accepting not only the rights but also the responsibilities and codes of good conduct implied by citizenship operate as a form of subjection rather than as an act of subversion, despite the claimant's (non) citizenship status. Obedience, discipline and good conduct are the results of these forms of subjection; exercising the power of the state upon oneself even when one's existence is negated, desiring the state despite the violence it exercises on people's lives. As Jack Halberstam (2013) argues in relation to the *undercommons*, in the refusal to be included and integrated within these enclosed fields of politics lies the possibility to 'shape desire, re-orient hope, re-imagine possibility and do so separate from the fantasies nestled into rights and responsibility' (12). Accordingly, we need to 'listen to the noise we make and refuse the offer we receive to make that noise music' (7).

Conclusions

By creating common and autonomous spaces and homes, migrants' squats resist and oppose state-led social engineering related to the organization of spatialities, temporal-ities, affects and lives, while also prefiguring societies and modes of existence that *escape* and *counter* the state and borders regimes. Namely, they open the possibility for radical subjectivities to be formed, which have the capacity to transform the very relations of power in which we constitute ourselves as citizens, and where everyday life is dis-ciplined, domesticated, and confined within specific modalities of experience (Revel 2009; Lazzarato 2009). This way politics of inhabitance are constituted, creating spaces where undocumented migrants' lives are not disciplined nor oppressed, and where border violence is not ameliorated but made visible and contested.

The creation of common squatted spaces outside of state control constitutes radical practices where the struggle is not formulated around demanding basic human rights but seeks to challenge the very foundations of racialized border regimes and their multiple forms of enclosure, be they securitarian or humanitarian. Rather than relying on assistance and the fulfilment of pre-defined rights, these struggles entail direct action for seizing freedom of movement, of inhabitance and of existence. When people live their lives in common, care does not come with control and instead constitutes a radical praxis of collective liberation. Therefore, the heterogeneous communities that emerge through housing squats not only resist and oppose borders, but produce forms of inhabitance that create conditions to live outside and against the modes of subjections engendered by migration control, citizenship politics, and humanitarian rhetoric and interventions.

Yet, while refusing basic rights and contesting the politics and affective technologies of humanitarian approaches, to some extent parts of the We Are Here movement had to accept government negotiations and compromises (temporary accommodations in former prisons, night shelters as solutions and cooperation on the revision of their status) and adopted more traditional forms of rights-claiming. Humanitarian discourses and forms of tolerance were used as a strategy of cooptation of those squats that constituted informal emergency shelters, while differentiating them from those squats that, instead of containing the 'problem', aimed at creating *cracks* (the latter were considered *political*, instead of humanitarian, and as such further criminalized). Moreover, the provision of shelter, food and basic rights through the BBB, reinforced the operation of border regimes by creating forms of dependency on charity and the benevolence of the state, and enclosed migrants' capacity to articulate collective voices and organize their struggles.

Thus, these technologies operated as a subtle technique of governmentality, coercing people to conduct themselves the way the government wishes them to, governing at a distance while masking the structural violence of these modes of subjection. However, these tactics did not succeed to contain the struggle in its entirety: many migrants rejected humanitarian solutions, continued to create radical home spaces through squatting, enacting a radical politics, ethics and *praxis* of inhabitance beyond citizenship.

Notes

1. http://curia.europa.eu/juris/document/document.jsf?docid=164725&doclang=EN
2. Translated from Dutch from: https://zoek.officielebekendmakingen.nl/kst-33512-3.html.
3. See Rutte's (the Dutch Prime Minister) response to Trump's inauguration. 'A letter to all Dutch citizens' https://vvd.nl/nieuws/lees-hier-de-brief-van-mark/.
4. Foucault's understanding of micro-physics of power, addresses technologies of government, devices, tools, techniques, and apparatuses that enable the shaping and acting upon individual and collective conduct (Foucault 1982). Foucault (2007) proposes the concept of conduct as translation of the Greek 'oikonomia psuchon and the Latin 'regimen animourum' (Foucault 2007, 192), namely, the way in which modes of government operate through management of souls insofar as this direction (conduite) of souls involves a permanent intervention on everyday conduct (conduite), on people's bodies and affects. In this context 'conduct' is a technique to lead others, but also the way one conducts oneself, a reflexive power on the self.
5. See: http://freedomnotfrontex.noblogs.org .
6. See: https://www.coe.int/en/web/turin-european-social-charter/processed-complaints/-/asset_publisher/5GEFkJmH2bYG/content/no-90-2013-conference-of-european-churches-cec-v-the-netherlands?inheritRedirect=false .
7. http://wijzijnhier.org/2014/11/.

Disclosure statement

No potential conflict of interest was reported by the author.

References

Aas, K. F. 2011. "'Crimmigrant'bodies and Bona Fide Travelers: Surveillance, Citizenship and Global Governance." *Theoretical Criminology* 15 (3): 331–346. doi:10.1177/1362480610396643.
Agier, M. 2011. *Managing the Undesirables*. Cambridge: Polity.
Ahmed, S. 2008. "The Politics of Good Feeling." *ACRAWSA E-Journal* 4 (1): 1–18.
Anderson, B., N. Sharma, and C. Wright. 2009. "Why No Borders?" *Refuge: Canada's Journal on Refugees* 26 (2): 5–18.

Ataç, I., K. Rygiel, and M. Stierl. 2016. "Introduction: The Contentious Politics of Refugee and Migrant Protest and Solidarity Movements: Remaking Citizenship from the Margins." *Citizenship Studies* 20 (5): 527–544. doi:10.1080/13621025.2016.1182681.

Balibar, É. 2009. "Europe as Borderland." *Environment and Planning D: Society and Space* 27 (2): 190–215. doi:10.1068/d13008.

Balibar, É. 2016. *Citizen Subject: Foundations for Philosophical Anthropology.* New York: Fordham University Press.

Bargetz, B. 2015. "The Distribution of Emotions: Affective Politics of Emancipation." *Hypatia* 30 (3): 580–596. doi:10.1111/hypa.2015.30.issue-3.

Bigo, D. 2014. "The (In) Securitization Practices of the Three Universes of EU Border Control: Military/Navy–Border Guards/Police–Database Analysts." *Security Dialogue* 45 (3): 209–225. doi:10.1177/0967010614530459.

Boler, M. 2004. *Feeling Power: Emotions and Education.* London: Routledge.

Brants, C. 1998. "The Fine Art of Regulated Tolerance: Prostitution in Amsterdam." *Journal of Law and Society* 25 (4): 621–635. doi:10.1111/jols.1998.25.issue-4.

Broeders, D. 2010. "Return to Sender? Administrative Detention of Irregular Migrants in Germany and the Netherlands." *Punishment & Society* 12 (2): 169–186. doi:10.1177/1462474509357375.

Brown, W. 2009. *Regulating Aversion: Tolerance in the Age of Identity and Empire.* Princeton: Princeton University Press.

Brun, C. 2015. "Active Waiting and Changing Hopes: Toward a Time Perspective on Protracted Displacement." *Social Analysis* 59 (1): 19–37. doi:10.3167/sa.2015.590102.

Brun, C. 2016. "There Is No Future in Humanitarianism: Emergency, Temporality and Protracted Displacement." *History and Anthropology* 27 (4): 393–410. doi:10.1080/02757206.2016.1207637.

Buruma, Y. 2007. "Dutch Tolerance: On Drugs, Prostitution, and Euthanasia." *Crime and Justice* 35 (1): 73–113. doi:10.1086/650185.

Butler, J. 1997. *The Psychic Life of Power: Theories in Subjection.* Redwood: Stanford University Press.

Cadman, L. 2010. "How (Not) to Be Governed: Foucault, Critique, and the Political." *Environment and Planning D: Society and Space* 28 (3): 539–556. doi:10.1068/d4509.

Clough, P. 2010. "Afterword: The Future of Affect Studies." *Body and Society* 16 (1): 222–230. doi:10.1177/1357034X09355302.

Clough, P., and J. Halley. 2007. *The Affective Turn: Theorizing the Social.* Durham: Duke University Press.

Cuttitta, P. 2018. "Delocalization, Humanitarianism, and Human Rights: The Mediterranean Border between Exclusion and Inclusion." *Antipode* 50 (3): 783–803. doi:10.1111/anti.2018.50.issue-3.

D'Aoust, A. M. 2014. "Ties that Bind? Engaging Emotions, Governmentality and Neoliberalism: Introduction to the Special Issue." *Global Society* 28 (3): 267–276. doi:10.1080/13600826.2014.900743.

Dadusc, D. 2016. "Squatting and the Undocumented Migrants Struggle in the Netherlands." Chap. 21 in *Migration, Squatting and Radical Autonomy,* edited by P. Mudu and S. Chattopadhyay, 275–284. London: Routledge.

Dadusc, D. 2019. "Enclosing Autonomy." *City* 23 (2): 1–19. doi:10.1080/13604813.2019.1615760.

Dadusc, D., M. Grazioli, and M. Martinez. 2019. "Citizenship as Inhabitance? Migrant Housing Squats versus Institutional Accommodation." *Citizenship Studies* 23: 6.

De Genova, N. P. 2002. "Migrant "Illegality" and Deportability in Everyday Life." *Annual Review of Anthropology* 31 (1): 419–447. doi:10.1146/annurev.anthro.31.040402.085432.

Fassin, D. 2011. *Humanitarian Reason: A Moral History of the Present.* Oakland: University of California Press.

Fortier, A. M. 2016. "Afterword: Acts of Affective Citizenship? Possibilities and Limitations." *Citizenship Studies* 20 (8): 1038–1044. doi:10.1080/13621025.2016.1229190.

Foucault, M. 1982. "The Subject and Power." *Critical Inquiry* 8 (4): 777–795. doi:10.1086/448181.

Foucault, M. 2007. *Security, Territory, Population: Lectures at the Collège De France, 1977–78*. Cham: Springer.

Gregg, M., and G. J. Seigworth, eds. 2010. *The Affect Theory Reader*. Durham: Duke University Press.

Halberstam, J. 2013. "The Wild Beyond: With and for the Undercommons." In *The Undercommons: Fugitive Planning and Black Study*, edited by F. Moten and S. Harney, 2–13. New York: Minor Compositions.

Hyndman, J. 2000. *Managing Displacement: Refugees and the Politics of Humanitarianism*. Minneapolis: University of Minnesota Press.

Hyndman, J., and W. Giles. 2011. "Waiting for What? the Feminization of Asylum in Protracted Situations." *Gender, Place and Culture* 18 (3): 361–379. doi:10.1080/0966369X.2011.566347.

Hynes, M. 2013. "Reconceptualizing Resistance: Sociology and the Affective Dimension of Resistance." *The British Journal of Sociology* 64 (4): 559–577. doi:10.1111/1468-4446.12038.

Ikizoglu Erensu, A. 2016. "Notes from a Refugee Protest: Ambivalences of Resisting and Desiring Citizenship." *Citizenship Studies* 20 (5): 664–677. doi:10.1080/13621025.2016.1182677.

Jones, R., and C. Johnson. 2016. *Placing the Border in Everyday Life*. London: Routledge.

Lazzarato, M. 2009. "Neoliberalism in Action: Inequality, Insecurity and the Reconstitution of the Social." *Theory, Culture and Society* 26 (6): 109–133. doi:10.1177/0263276409350283.

Leerkes, A., and D. Broeders. 2010. "A Case of Mixed Motives?: Formal and Informal Functions of Administrative Immigration Detention." *The British Journal of Criminology* 50 (5): 830–850. doi:10.1093/bjc/azq035.

Leerkes, A., G. Engbersen, and J. Van der Leun. 2012. "Crime among Irregular Immigrants and the Influence of Internal Border Control." *Crime, Law and Social Change* 58 (1): 15–38. doi:10.1007/s10611-012-9367-0.

Mezzadra, S. 2015. "The Proliferation of Borders and the Right to Escape." In *The Irregularization of Migration in Contemporary Europe: Detention, Deportation, Drowning*, edited by Y. Jansen, R. Celikates, and J. De Bloois, 121–135. London: Rowman & Littlefield International.

Mudu, P., and S. Chattopadhyay, eds. 2017. *Migration, Squatting and Radical Autonomy: Resistance and Destabilization of Racist Regulatory Policies and B/Ordering Mechanisms*. New York: Routledge.

Nigg, H. 2015. "Sans-Papiers on Their March for Freedom 2014: How Refugees and Undocumented Migrants Challenge Fortress Europe." *Interface: A Journal on Social Movements* 7: 1.

Nyers, P. 2013. *Rethinking Refugees: Beyond State of Emergency*. London: Routledge.

Pallister-Wilkins, P. 2018. "Hotspots and the Geographies of Humanitarianism." *Environment and Planning D: Society and Space*, 1–18. doi:10.1177/0263775818754884

Pallister-Wilkins, P. 2015. "The Humanitarian Politics of European Border Policing: Frontex and Border Police in Evros." *International Political Sociology* 9 (1): 53–69. doi:10.1111/ips.2015.9.issue-1.

Papadopoulos, D., N. Stephenson, and V. Tsianos. 2008. *Escape Routes. Control and Subversion in the 21st Century*. London – Ann Arbor, MI: Pluto Press.

Papadopoulos, D., and V. Tsianos. 2013. "After Citizenship: Autonomy of Migration, Organisational Ontology and Mobile Commons." *Citizenship Studies* 17 (2): 178–196. doi:10.1080/13621025.2013.780736.

Pedwell, C. 2012. "Affective (Self-) Transformations: Empathy, Neoliberalism and International Development." *Feminist Theory* 13 (2): 163–179. doi:10.1177/1464700112442644.

Pedwell, C., and A. Whitehead. 2012. "Affecting Feminism: Questions of Feeling in Feminist Theory." *Feminist Theory* 13 (2): 115–129. doi:10.1177/1464700112442635.

Read, J. 2003. *The Micro-Politics of Capital: Marx and the Prehistory of the Present*. New York: SUNY Press.

Revel, J. 2009. "Identity, Nature, Life: Three Biopolitical Deconstructions." *Theory, Culture and Society* 26 (6): 45–54. doi:10.1177/0263276409348854.

Rigby, J., and R. Schlembach. 2013. "Impossible Protest: Noborders in Calais." *Citizenship Studies* 17 (2): 157–172. doi:10.1080/13621025.2013.780731.

Rygiel, K. 2011. "Bordering Solidarities: Migrant Activism and the Politics of Movement and Camps at Calais." *Citizenship Studies* 15 (1): 1–19. doi:10.1080/13621025.2011.534911.

Salter, M. B. 2006. "The Global Visa Regime and the Political Technologies of the International Self: Borders, Bodies, Biopolitics." *Alternatives* 31 (2): 167–189. doi:10.1177/030437540603100203.

Squire, V. 2016. *The Exclusionary Politics of Asylum*. London: Springer.

Squire, V., and J. Darling. 2013. "The "Minor" Politics of Rightful Presence: Justice and Relationality in City of Sanctuary." *International Political Sociology* 7 (1): 59–74. doi:10.1111/ips.2013.7.issue-1.

Starling, R. 2015. "Niemand Slaapt Bij Ons Op Straat? over De Noodopvang Van Onrechtmatig Verblijvende Vreemdelingen En Het Steekspel Tussen Centrale Overheid En Gemeenten." *Justitiële Verkenningen* 41 (2): 24–37. doi:10.5553/JV/016758502015041002003.

Stierl, M. 2018. *Migrant Resistance in Contemporary Europe: Resistance as Method*. London: Routledge.

Stumpf, J. 2006. "The Crimmigration Crisis: Immigrants, Crime, and Sovereign Power." *American University Law Review* 56 (2): 367–419.

Tazzioli, M. 2014. *Spaces of Governmentality*. London: Rowman & Littlefield International.

Ticktin, M. 2016. "Thinking beyond Humanitarian Borders." *Social Research: An International Quarterly* 83 (2): 255–271.

Tweede Kamer der Staten-Generaal. 2013. vergaderjaar 2012–2013, 33 512, nr. 2 1.

Van der Leun, J. 2006. "Excluding Illegal Migrants in the Netherlands: Between National Policies and Local Implementation." *West European Politics* 29 (2): 310–326. doi:10.1080/01402380500512650.

Van der Leun, J., and R. Kloosterman. 2006. "Going Underground: Immigration Policy Changes and Shifts in Modes of Provision of Undocumented Immigrants in the Netherlands." *Tijdschrift Voor Economische En Sociale Geografie* 97 (1): 59–68. doi:10.1111/tesg.2006.97.issue-1.

Van der Woude, M. A., J. P. van der Leun, and J. A. A. Nijland. 2014. "Crimmigration in the N Etherlands." *Law and Social Inquiry* 39 (3): 560–579. doi:10.1111/lsi.12078.

Vaughan-Williams, N. 2008. "Borderwork beyond Inside/Outside? Frontex, the Citizen–Detective and the War on Terror." *Space and Polity* 12 (1): 63–79. doi:10.1080/13562570801969457.

Vaughan-Williams, N. 2015. ""We are Not Animals!" Humanitarian Border Security and Zoopolitical Spaces in EUrope." *Political Geography* 45: 1–10. doi:10.1016/j.polgeo.2014.09.009.

Walters, W. 2010. "Foucault and Frontiers: Notes on the Birth of the Humanitarian Border." In *Governmentality: Current Issues and Future Challenges*, edited by U. Bröckling, S. Krasmann, and T. Lemke, 146–172. London: Routledge.

Weizman, E. 2011. *The Least of All Possible Evils: Humanitarian Violence from Arendt to Gaza*. London: Verso Books.

Bordering through domicide: spatializing citizenship in Calais

Travis Van Isacker

ABSTRACT
This paper examines domicidal practices against illegalized border crossers in Calais, France as a technology of citizenship and migration governance. It addresses recent calls to include actions and interventions which restrict citizenship in the context of illegalized migration within critical citizenship studies literature. Studying the state violence upholding and spatializing normative citizenship allows for a deeper understanding of citizenship's implication in the European border regime, and raises questions on the concept's continued application to theorizations of migrants' political movements and spatial manifestations. The paper proposes anti-citizen politics as an alternative before arguing that the presence of this politics within the city's squats and jungles, more than the physical occupations as such, is what the French state seeks to eradicate through acts of domicide. Working from empirical examples, the article describes a 'carrot-and-stick' domicide currently at work in Calais where the eviction and destruction of autonomous forms of migrant inhabitance is combined with a simultaneous offer of state managed accommodation. These tactics operate together to drive migrants out of the city of Calais, away from the UK border, and ultimately into a determination of their detain/deport-ability via citizenship's scrutiny.

1. Introduction: acts of exclusion

Illegalized migrants taking space in their daily movements resisting and subverting the European border regime has lead to intense debate on the implications for contemporary notions of citizenship. Recent special issues within this journal (see 20.5 Ataç, Rygiel, and Stierl (2016) and 21.6 Maestri and Hughes (2017)) have highlighted how these actions spatially constitute substantive citizenship and undermine citizenship's strict conception as a legal category determining political existence within a territory. Throughout these discussions runs a tension between 'migrant citizenship' scholarship and the 'autonomy of migration' perspective (Nyers 2015). The former reads migrant spatial ruptures and contentious inhabitance into the politics of citizenship to complicate the concept, while the latter instead reads them through 'the commons'. Although differing in their conclusions as to whether migrants' occupations and protests should be incorporated into the language and politics of citizenship, the two analytical veins share a methodological approach; interrogating citizenship from the perspective of illegalized migrants' struggles to move and stay as they please.

This article takes a slightly different tack. Rather than analyzing citizenship through migrants' spatial ruptures and forms of contentious inhabitance, it instead looks at how the state reacts to these ruptures, how those reactions reinforce normative citizenship, and how citizenship itself functions as a tool of migration control within the context of Calais, France. It responds to calls by Fortier (2016) and Darling (2017) to produce analyses of actions which delimit citizenship and further entrench it as a condition of the privileged few within critical citizenship studies. While the literature spawned by 'acts of citizenship' (Isin and Nielsen 2008) which Fortier and Darling address celebrates migrant activism as the motor of a progressive drive towards egalitarian citizenship (perhaps even an unbordered future), we must keep in mind citizenship's continued role as a primary tool for control of human mobility. Therefore, studies explicating 'techniques of govern-mentality deployed by states' which reestablish a normative and exclusionary definition of citizenship (Fortier 2016, 1040), as well as those 'spaces formed around exclusionary acts of citizenship' which 'are actively *destructive* of other ways of being' (Darling 2017, 734) are urgently needed. A critical understanding of the ways citizenship is used to govern migration not only shows how and by whom citizenship becomes restricted, but raises further questions on the techniques of capture present within citizenship itself while suggesting ways to subvert them.

The argument here then concerns itself with the citizenship of the police, in both real and Rancièrian terms, less than the (citizenship) politics of those struggling for the freedom of all to move and stay throughout Europe. Recognizing citizenship as historically an important imperial technology of subjugation and mobility control (Hindess 2004) as well as it's current inability to grasp the full political significance of contemporary migrations given its coloniality (Vázquez in Ansems de Vries et al. 2017, 8–9), this paper echoes calls for scholars to break with methodological citizenship in their analyzes of migration politics (Papadopoulos and Tsianos 2013; Tazzioli 2017a). However, citizenship nevertheless remains key to understanding state strategies and technologies of migration governance. Contrasting with the other papers in this special issue which show how migrants' squats, other contentious occupations, and their home-making practices illustrate political and spatial praxes which go beyond citizenship, I'd like to understand how and why these forms of inhabitance are evicted and destroyed. What is the state's strategy behind the domicide of migrant living spaces in Calais, how does domicide function as a political technology of citizenship, and how does state domicide contribute to establishing the citizenship regime as a fundamental technique of contemporary European migration governance?

Beginning by revisiting recent discussions on citizenship, space, and migration, a working conception of citizenship as a normative and exclusionary concept will be established before turning to how political contestations of citizenship manifest spatially. Building on the work of other geographers in the field (Mould 2017a,b), the second theoretical portion of the article establishes domicide as a political tech-nology of citizenship fundamental to the state strategy of migration control in Calais. It functions by eliminating spaces in which people live their lives beyond and against citizenship's jurisdiction while channeling autonomous migrations into 'spaces of citizenship' where they can be captured and/or redirected into the state controlled circuits of mobility. Beginning with domicide's initial definition taken from Douglas and Smith (2001) as the deliberate destruction of home, criticisms and refinements will be made to the concept before applying it to the eviction and destruction of migrant living spaces in Calais. While there has been wide scholarly interest in migrant's spatial protests, the eviction, destruction, and erasure of those spaces remain understudied.

The second portion of the article illustrates how domicide functions in Calais by presenting empirical examples; the evictions creating the large jungle existing between Summer 2015 and Fall 2016, the multiple evictions and relocations of the inhabitants of a women and children's squat in 2014, and the current hyperactive campaign of domicide being waged against any form of shelter established by migrants in the city. These examples provide a broad impression of how domicide takes place in Calais across time, scale, and with different tactics, while showing how in each case the common goal remained the segregation of Calais' urban space as one of European citizenship, the spatial exclusion or containment of 'non-citizens', the gradual filtering of those 'non-citizens' into state controlled spaces of citizenship, and the elimination of autonomous spaces which undermined the citizenship regime.

2. Spatializing citizenship and anti-citizen politics in Calais

While citizenship can perhaps best be defined as a site of contest constituted by the struggle over it (Balibar 2009), this research focuses on one half of that struggle; the reterritorialization of the autonomous spaces 'non-citizens' inhabit by the state in its defense of citizenship. Here I deliberately mobilize a specific exclusionary and normative conception of the term. It is a recognizably limited understanding of citizenship; however, as the focus here is not on its content (the rights and responsibilities citizenship entails), nor how it can be expanded to encompass other-than-citizen political actions, this conception is nonetheless appropriate. The argument takes the state's own restrictive, though still hegemonic, definition to explore the production of 'non-citizen' spatial exclusion rather than work to redefine citizenship or discovering qualities attributed to it at work in the political mobilizations of the excluded.

Furthermore, the spatial perspective taken here refrains from speculating on others' political subjectivities, and focuses on the space and materiality of how citizenship is constituted, maintained, and mobilized in migration control strategies. Imagining citizenship as a tangible web distributed over space and imposing upon it a normative geometry of interactive possibilities denaturalizes spaces of abjection, and denormalizes the distinctions between classes of inhabitants. The writing of citizenship's logic into space *orients* people to or away from each other based upon the distance and arrangement of objects which make it up, and acts to restrict the possibilities and types of encounters within and across (non/citizen) groups (Isin 2002, 48–49). How bodies are arranged within space, the distances placed between them, and what spaces certain bodies are allowed to inhabit or are removed from according to the logic and distinctions inscribed by citizenship are political contestations imbued with histories of systematic domination and exclusion that become written into environments and then materially reinforced by them. While this article is principally focused on elaborating exactly how domicide is used to spatialize and materially enforce normative citizenship in Calais, it is first relevant to briefly explore the politics of migrant spatial inhabitance in rupturing citizenship, and how they pose an existential threat to it as governmental logic.

There have been a number of recent studies highlighting the importance of space in ordering and rupturing citizenship through examples of migrant struggles. Most recently, *Contested spaces of citizenship* argued citizenship *is* spatial because technologies and strategies of exclusion against 'non-citizens' are spatially manifested, and because taking space is a fundamental act by which migrants contest exclusion and demand (citizenship) rights (Maestri and Hughes 2017, 628). Space is shown to be an important factor within migrant struggles at many levels; from the choice of protest location to how that protest interacts with the space in which it takes place (Ataç, Rygiel, and Stierl 2016, 538). This is not to mention most migrant protest actions are organized around the subversion and disruption of a decidedly spatial strategy of governmental control of movement, or their outright spatial exclusion through deportation or detention (Ataç, Rygiel, and Stierl 2016). However, beyond the appropriation of space within protest, the contentious *inhabitance* of space (be it through squatting buildings, occupying infrastructure or symbolic locations, or establishing and defending autonomous encampments) carries additional implications.

The contentious inhabitance of space amplifies the visibility of occupant's grievances, asserts the occupants as political subjects, and creates space and time for solidarities to develop across citizenship categories (see the other articles in the issue as well as Ataç (2016) and Mudu and Chattopadhyay (2017)). In Calais, squatted spaces established and shared by coalitions of illegalized migrants crossing to the UK, asylum seekers in France, European passport holders, and local Calaisiens went beyond providing material support to migrants in precarious living situations and created links of solidarity and mutual aid 'as people struggled together against police brutality and repressive border control mechanisms' (Calais Migrant Solidarity 2017, 62–63). Calais Migrant Solidarity describe how hunger strikes were organized and supported, evictions resisted, future squatting actions organized, locals politicized and radicalized, and information spread on navigating the British asylum system all from the personal relationships developed within just one of these squats. King (2016, 125) describes how these spaces 'built bridges between people with and without papers … [and] amounted to an experiment in equality that was also another way of being outside the state'. These experiments in 'being outside the state' as well as many of the concrete activities that took place in the squats of Calais represent what in this paper will tentatively be termed a politics of anti-citizenship.

This concept can be thought alongside (but goes beyond) the 'no border' politics sketched by Anderson, Sharma, and Wright (2009, 2012) and King (2016) among others. It is the practical and everyday refusal to reinforce citizenship as a mechanism of bordering and exclusion by redefining relationships of cooperation and solidarity without reference to citizenship categories. It is a politics of coalition comprising people positioned across various categories of (non)citizenship status who together develop collective actions aimed at eliminating citizenship's arbitrary juridical distinctions and the privileges stemming them. It is performed both when those excluded from citizenship act in defiance of their exclusions and when those holding citizenship privileges mobilize them against the border regime and its underlying citizenship logic. Not a superficial opposition to citizenship, anti-citizen politics begins with deeply engaging the lived realities of inequality produced by citizenship's exclusions and differential inclusions whilst working towards their dismantlement. It is not prescriptive or didactic but is sensitive to migrants' strategic appropriations of citizenship to win material gains while remaining concerned with prefiguring spaces, structures, and mobilities outside and against citizenship.

The crucial difference between anti-citizenship politics and 'acts of citizenship' (Isin and Nielsen 2008) or 'citizenship from below' (Nyers and Rygiel 2012, 9) is, whilst similarly breaking from citizenship's primacy in determining who or what actions are allowed to count as political, anti-citizen politics actively seeks to undo citizenship. It focuses on collectively subverting and challenging its technologies (e.g. borders, detention, deportation, enforced destitution) while refusing to reproduce its categories in the movement's organizing and aims. Theoretically, a politics of anti-citizenship recognizes not only that it is impossible to separate citizenship from its juridical status and function of mobility control (De Genova 2017, 20), but also that every argument to expand citizenship rights is premised upon the deferred exclusion of another. As Amy Brandzel writes, '[t]here is no such thing as a movement of citizenship and inclusion for *some* that does not further the vulnerability and disenfranchisement of *others*' (2016, x). Even when fighting for the widest possible inclusion, the logic of citizenship requires breaking apart wider solidarities across demographic or citizenship status categories: for example between 'Europeans' and 'migrants'; 'refugees', 'asylum seekers' and 'economic migrants'; or amongst countries of origin. There is a fundamental discord in establishing a politics of freedom to move and stay for all in citizenship rights, and perhaps instead we must begin this task by squarely opposing citizenship as subjectivity, political practice, and ultimate horizon.

I do not contend that anti-citizen politics is present in all actions targeting the border regime in Calais – indeed Rigby and Schlembach have shown how even during the 2009 No Border camp citizenship remained 'a way of defining and policing the borders of who and what could count as political' (2013, 158). Nor do I argue all forms of autonomous migrant inhabitance in the city necessarily manifest such politics – there exists an extremely complex and often ambiguous relationship between the spaces migrants end up calling home, segregation, exclusion, political resistance, and citizenship in Calais.[1] Instead, I want to focus on the ways in which Calais' squats and jungles *spatialize* anti-citizenship politics, and then, more specifically, how and why they are targeted for elimination through state domicide. Indeed, although Mezzadra and Neilson would no doubt argue against an anti-citizen politics as it has been offered here – preferring instead to interrogate the 'frame and discourse of citizenship' than abandon it (2013, 261) – in their critique of No Borders they do laud the *political spaces* which have been opened up by its movements, and which are the subject here (268). These spaces enable anti-citizen politics across and against citizenship's distinctions by incubating their occupants from intrusion by the citizenship regime as represented by the police or access controls based on biometric registration or an asylum claim, and often exist to directly facilitate unauthorized border crossings. To the extent they refuse to reproduce, while providing a toe-hold from which to collectively resist, citizenship's fundamental distinctions and mechanisms of mobility control, these spaces could be said to possess an anti-citizen quality which becomes the ultimate target for elimination by the state.

3. Refining domicide

Geographers Porteous and Smith (2001, 19) initially theorized domicide as the 'planned deliberate destruction of home causing suffering to the dweller'. Thinking the elimination of anti-citizen spaces of inhabitance through domicide highlights the erasure as an act of violence committed by intentional actors who stand to profit, implement their ideological positions, or consolidate political power while representing these consequences as being for 'the common good' (184). Framing the evictions and destructions in Calais through domicide counters the paternalistic humanitarian narratives through which they are often justified by authorities. However, this initial definition must be refined to include the more nuanced ways domicide functions as a spatial technology of citizenship and migration governance in Calais.

For Porteous and Smith the material loss of home and the victim's resultant experience of suffering is the measure by which eviction is considered domicide (2001, 192). This criteria makes it difficult to recognize more nuanced tactics *as* domicide; perhaps where coercion or incentive is used so people 'willingly' leave their homes. There must be an expansion of the concept to encompass evictions which do not become spectacles as violent erasures nevertheless. Particularly in Calais where a 'carrot-and-stick' strategy is used, it is imperative to recognize actions which eventually result in the elimination of forms of anti-citizen inhabitance as domicide. In doing so, responsibility is attributed to the state actors who reassert citizenship status as determining one's right to inhabit the city through enacting domicide, and spatial exclusion, against 'non-citizens'.

Furthermore, the threshold of suffering in Porteous and Smith's original definition must also be reappraised. In their articulation domicide requires a persistent subjective experience of pain and mourning. However, groups of evictees are not homogeneous and amongst them there can be multiple attitudes towards the loss of a home, with some perhaps welcoming it. For example, some residents saw the eviction of 'The Jungles' in October 2016 as an opportunity to move to a more hospitable city or improve the material conditions of their lives in France. However, the implications of the removals greatly benefited the politicians' goal of eliminating migrant forms of inhabitance in Calais rather than provide a good faith solution to 'non-citizen's' accommodation needs, and even before the final evictions, many of those who left 'The Jungle' in 2016 chose to return after seeing that the alternatives they were sent to were not fit for their needs (Calais Writers 2017, 248).

The measure of suffering in Porteous and Smiths' original definition further victimizes targets of domicide, and limits the understandings and consequences of their resistant solidarities (Nowicki 2014, 791). Implying those removed from their homes can only, even requiring they must, suffer minimizes or altogether discounts direct acts of resistance and the personal empowerment generated by them. For example, again during 'The Jungle's' 2016 eviction, some residents decided to set their own homes on fire in protest rather than see them dismantled by state contracted workers (Calais Migrant Solidarity 2016). This example severely disturbs the position Porteous and Smith's definition gives to targets of domicide, as well as the victimizing narratives in which they are framed. Despite the superficial paradox of inhabitants spectacularly destroying their own dwellings in protest of the planned demolitions, these actions can be understood as mobilizing the limited means jungle residents had to resist given the overwhelming number of police present, and as a powerful refusal to reproduce the eviction's non-violent veneer. By setting fire to their homes the residents showed that the eviction *was* violent despite massive state efforts to prevent it being mediatized as such. In a bizarre and insulting attempt to maintain this facade even after the fires had begun, the Prefet of Nord/Pas-de-Calais, Fabienne Buccio, described the burning as a tradition the migrants had of setting their homes alight before departing (Reuters 2016).

Apart from the eviction and material destruction of existing homes, domicide must also be recognized as the denial of homebuilding capacities. In Calais this has taken the form of police preventing volunteers from bringing in more durable materials like stone or brick which could be used to create permanent dwellings in 'The Jungle' (Mould 2017b, 7); police harassing and interrogating members of an aid association while they were distributing tents following an eviction in 2018 (Délinquants Solidaires 2018); and a continuous attempt from the city's mayor, Natasha Bouchart, to criminalize squatting in France (Le Figaro 2015). These are just three examples of attempts to remove the capacity of people to create autonomous forms of inhabitance, while also preempting the need for large scale and recognizably violent evictions and destructions. With domicide in Calais being made increasingly routine and invisible, it is imperative to continue recognizing and resisting all actions which are part of a domicidal strategy to prevent illegalized migrants from constructing shelters that contribute to the homeliness of space and the security of their inhabitance (Mould 2017a, 13).

Given the above criticisms, I will employ a strictly spatial definition of domicide as the intentional elimination of contentious spaces and forms of inhabitance. This is primarily by their material destruction, but also occurs through more opaque techniques (like coerced abandonment or actions which prevent development). Limiting the measure to whether or not an action contributes to the spatial erasure of inhabitance gestures towards the affective implications of erasure, but does not prescribe how those whose homes are being destroyed should experience the event or respond to it.

Domicide functions as a technology of citizenship both by physically destroying 'undesired' dwellings and by socio-symbolically prescribing normative forms of spatial inhabitance and citizenship (Nowicki 2017, 172). Within Calais, the destruction of 'non-citizen's' homes in the city segregates illegalized people beyond its territory and forces them to live in near invisibility, with often no more than the semblance of a shelter, and where they are heavily targeted by policing operations in an effort to exhaust and expel them further. Additionally, domicide is aims at breaking apart anti-citizen communities and friendships of solidarity in resistance to the border/citizenship regime (Mould 2017b, 7). Although a fundamentally important technology through which normative citizenship is maintained and human mobility controlled, domicide has increasingly become just one half of the state's strategy in Calais next to the enclosure of the evictees within spaces of citizenship.

4. Domicide as technology of citizenship in Calais, France

4.1. Calais' border

Before detailing recent examples of domicide in Calais it is useful to briefly recount the history of its border and the consistent denial of migrant accommodation. Situated approximately fifty kilometers from the South-East Coast of Britain, Calais is the closest port to the United Kingdom. The Calais – Dover ferry crossings are the shortest and cheapest not to mention the Eurotunnel terminal which transports passengers and freight under the seabed in less than an hour. The ease with which commodities and those holding proper documents pass through the city's ports and onto the ships and trains bound for the UK contrasts sharply with the militarized infrastructure in place to prevent unauthorized persons from making the crossing. Most who cross the channel clandestinely from Calais do so by attaching themselves to these logistical flows, trying to not be recognized as an out-of-place human body amidst the tons of cargo and innumerable vehicles permitted to traverse the narrow waterway each day.

Calais, although on the European mainland, essentially became the territorial boundary of the UK with the signing of the Le Touquet treaty in 2003. This agreement established juxtaposed immigration controls on cross-channels ferry routes following an existing arrangement on crossings made through the Eurotunnel. This externalization of the UK border has made Calais into a choke point for migratory flows to the UK, with illegalized migrants being forced to spend months living precariously in the city whilst making their own attempts to cross clandestinely. Between 1999 and 2002 there was an accommodation center managed by the Red Cross for illegalized border crossers in Sangatte (a small town next to Calais). There they could stay and rest in between attempts, have basic needs met, and not be pursued by police or threatened with arrest while doing so. However, this center was closed down after a sustained media campaign in the British press which portrayed it as having a 'magnet effect' and being a 'pull factor' encouraging and facilitating irregular crossings into Britain (Buchanan and Grillo 2004). The campaign has continued to effect the rhetoric surrounding migrant accommodation in Calais with politicians still defending proposals against accusations of creating 'a new Sangatte' (Vincent 2014).

The closure of the Red Cross center in Sangatte did not stop people from traveling to Calais to try and cross to the UK, but rather pushed them into less visible and more precarious spaces of inhabitance during the time they spend there. With nowhere else to stay, migrants began living in autonomous squats and jungles in much larger numbers. These settlements would continue to grow, and again became large enough to attract the attention of the UK media in the late 2000s. In 2009 there was a rush of security infrastructure spending for the port of Calais from the UK, while on the French side the Minister of Interior and recently elected anti-migrant Mayor Natasha Bouchart evicted and bulldozed around 800 people from the Pashtun Jungle despite their resistance (Calais Research 2017). Again, this eviction did not prevent people from returning to Calais to make their attempts to cross. In the following years the numbers of illegalized border crossers would grow again, and the squats and camps would continue to proliferate.

Between 2009 and 2015 many squats and jungles existed in and around the city. These were often spaces established and primarily occupied by people seeking to cross to the

UK (although there were also inhabited by people in various stages of regularizing their status in France as well as European passport holders). They were heavily targeted by French police, with raids, identity controls, arrests, and eviction, destruction, and re-occupation a constant cycle of life in them. Following the large number of arrivals in Summer 2014, a series of evictions and destructions around the city resulted in the consolidation of most of the migrant population in a single large encampment for the first time since Sangatte. Whilst this occupation was but one of the many jungles that have existed in the city, its size and visibility meant it was again exceptionally mediatized in the UK and eventually evicted and destroyed. Yet, continuing the repetitive cycle, after 'The Jungle' was obliterated and its inhabitants dispersed in October 2016, people continue returning to Calais to attempt their clandestine crossings, and now faced the most hyper-active and sustained campaign of domicide the city has ever seen.

4.2. The 'carrot and stick' of domicide and state accommodation

Calais is a site where territorial exclusion from the UK and intense internal migration policing in France converge. People presumed to be threatening the UK's border (often based on their living in autonomous spaces) are targeted in acts of domicide as a way to direct them into state managed 'accommodation'; either the detention centers or to the 'reception and orientation centers' – Centres d'accueil et d'orientation (CAO). The latter is for those who choose to claim asylum in France whilst the former for those who refuse. These places require people to be filtered and processed upon entrance by state bureaucracy in accordance with the citizenship regime in order to determine their deportability or detainability (De Genova 2007).

The provision of accommodation by the state depending upon or directing into an asylum claim (and often an eventual rejection) is merely the other side of the domicidal policies against autonomous migrant living spaces in Calais. While in previous years there were no accommodation solutions for evicted migrants (the local government always hoped they would just leave the city once their homes were destroyed), now the violent destructions are taken as an opportunity to bring evictees within 'spaces of citizenship'. Martina Tazzioli (2017b) describes this shift in tactic as 'expulsions of humanitarianism'; quoting one NGO worker as saying 'it is an eviction that is con-ducted for the benefit of the migrants, that is for transferring them into the circuits of the hosting system'. Despite this humanitarian veneer it is important to still recognize such evictions *as* domicide implicated within the wider border and citizenship regimes, and a fundamental node in the system of mobility control.

Carrot-and-stick domicide – eviction and destruction alongside inclusion within 'spaces of citizenship' – is the primary way in which citizenship is today spatialized in Calais. Those spaces which provide refuge outside of the citizenship regime, foster solidarities against and despite citizenship, and which carve out spaces for people to live autonomously beyond the detention centers or asylum seeker accommodation are targeted for elimination.

The policy of governing the city's migrant population through this 'carrot-and-stick' is acknowledged at the highest levels. French President Macron put it bluntly when stating migrants should understand '[t]o stay in Calais and build makeshift shelters or squats is a dead end. The alternative is clear; people can get to the reception centres where everyone's case will be examined and those who have the right, given asylum in our country' (Willsher 2018). These statements have provided the political and ideological justification for France's current extreme campaign of domicide in Calais following the eviction of the Jungle in October 2016. A report by the French Ministry of Interior shows that between May and August 2017 eighty 'anti-squat' operations took place, resulting in 195 destroyed occupations, and a total of 91,000 kilograms of destroyed belongings including shelter material, clothes, and other personal effects (Diaz et al. 2017, 32) while human rights observers counted 393 separate eviction operations between November 2017 and November 2018 (L'Auberge des Migrants, Utopia 56, Help Refugees, and Refugee Info Bus 2018). Currently, police visit and destroy migrant occupations multiple times per week, collecting and throwing away any objects which are left in the area after people have fled (Refugee Info Bus 2018a,b,c). These actions reflect the obsession within both local and national government to achieve 'zero squats in Calais' after the eviction of 'The Jungle' in 2016 alongside a paranoia towards the development of *points de fixation* – essentially any location where migrants are visible in the city or where they are able to access services.

This campaign of domicide is part of what has been called a wider 'politics of exhaustion' (Ansems de Vries and Welander 2016) operating against migrants in Calais and other European borderzones. Through a combination of uncertainty, enforced mobility (e.g. eviction, harassment, and deportation) and immobility (e.g. detention and waiting) it aims to break human bodies and spirits so that migrants opt themselves for abandoning further unregulated movement; that they recognize the 'dead end'. In Calais, the constant destruction of the material infrastructure needed for survival as well as the daily evictions keeping migrants on the move within police dictated circuits of mobility points to Macron's 'alternative' of moving to a state managed center as the only way out. With autonomous modes of inhabitance constantly being violently erased, the desires of the French state are clear; enter into the spatial circuits of citizenship, submit to the scrutiny of the asylum and regularization process here, and forgo an onward journey to the UK.

As briefly mentioned, this current provision of state accommodation alongside the enactment of domicide is a relatively new development in the state's migration control strategy. In the following examples it will be shown how domicide has been used previously to spatially segregate the migrant population and exclude them from the city. Looking at the creation of 'The Jungle' through two concurrent domicidal processes (one of a squat providing migrant family accommodation and the other of all other squats and jungles in the city), the following cases show how domicide operated to reinforce normative forms of spatial inhabitance based upon citizenship status, and was mobilized against spaces nurturing anti-citizenship solidarities.

4.3. The long domicide of the women and children's house

The women and children's shelter began as a squat within Calais' city center and was originally squatted by people with citizenship privileges in 2014. It was maintained as an autonomous space for most of its existence, in conflict with local government and the courts, and with no budget except for donations collected to pay for water, electricity, and gas. The squat was managed collectively by the women and their families, European residents with citizenship privileges, local neighbors, and other visitors from Calais. The residents lost their legal right to occupy the building with a court decision on November 19th, 2013 (Calais Migrant Solidarity 2013a) although the Prefect stated the police would not immediately act to evict the building (Calais Migrant Solidarity 2013b).

This decision to not evict was perhaps because the migrants housed were predominantly women and children, and the squat was receiving a lot of local support. Instead the Prefecture engaged the squatters in a negotiation regarding the occupation. While the ensuing discussions represented a significant shift in the way the state approached a squat in Calais, the threat of a violent eviction still loomed over the residents (King 2016, 114). The state's conditions were that only migrant women and children were allowed inside, and its current European residents would have to leave the squat to allow a contracted NGO to take it over. If these conditions were refused, the prefect said that the responsibility for the ensuing eviction would be on those Europeans who squatted the building and began the project for refusing to leave. Whilst not an uncontested decision, the non-migrant residents eventually left the squat and the NGO workers moved in.

Overnight this changed the lives of all the squat's residents and took away the social and communal (if not physical) space which had been shared and struggled for together over the last year. Furthermore, it brought an autonomous space under state control and ensured, through the introduction of state contracted NGO workers, the future evictions of the remaining residents would be easier. With this first eviction the state's target was less the occupation or the migrant residents themselves, but rather the anti-citizen politics found inside the squatted house which came from the solidarities amongst European and migrant squatters. At the time it was a space existing within the urban city center of Calais, but which explicitly refused to reproduce the spacial segregation of 'non-citizen' people in the city. The residents sought to establish equality amongst themselves based on a sensitivity to how life in Calais remained very different for each of them (King 2016, 110–115). A main purpose of the squat was to enable crossing attempts, and so the women were free to come and go through the night, and stay as they pleased without external conditions being placed on them or restricting their access. When taking over the running of the squat the state made the concession of not fingerprinting the residents and still letting them come and go throughout the night, but still saw an opportunity to filter the residents into the citizenship regime in ways which hadn't existed before by charging NGO workers to register and establish the situation of each of each person living inside and then report on it (La Voix du Nord 2014b). Furthermore, the state proposed women and children should only be able to stay for two months before being directed to 'more appropriate solutions' (La Voix du Nord 2014a).

After taking physical control of the site and introducing a contracted NGO to manage it, the government still had to remove the remaining inhabitants and end the contentious occupation. It was a big contradiction for the state to contract an NGO to work inside of a space which had been autonomously reclaimed, and whose occupation was deemed illegal by the court. Thus came the task of finding another location to house the remaining residents. The first building proposed was located in Calais-Nord, the historic city center. Natasha Bouchart intervened in order to prevent this;

specifically citing the close proximity of this location to both the food and clothing distribution areas, and because it was in the middle of Calais-Nord 'where there are already many problems with the migrants' (La Voix du Nord 2014a). Instead, she unilaterally requisitioned a space belonging to another NGO five kilometers away from the center to house them (La Voix du Nord 2014a). The women and children did not want to move there, but were forced to against their will. They were to be excluded from the city center, and the social networks and services it contained. The residents would again be forced to move into the Jules Ferry Centre in late March 2015 when the state began creating 'The Jungle' after nearly another year in this second location. Again, this was not what they wanted for themselves, but they were forced to under threat of police violence (Calais Migrant Solidarity 2015a). The NGO workers managing the project also encouraged them to go at each point, ensuring the domicides would proceed smoothly and be unnoticed.

The repeated and invisible acts of domicide against the women constituted the enclosure of anti-citizen spatial ruptures, and was the beginning of the segregation of most of almost all of Calais' illegalized border crossers as will be shown in the next section. At each moment the threat of police violence was used, if not directly enacted. However, these evictions did not take place without violence but were violent in and of themselves. They broke apart anti-citizen solidarities and interpersonal relationships, they uprooted families and thrust them into unknown locations further and further from the city center, and allowed the state regime of citizenship to enter into their lives by imposing conditions and time-limits upon access to a sleeping space.

4.4. Creating 'the jungle'

It was around the Jules Ferry Centre now housing the women and families that 'The Jungle' was to be constructed. While April 5th, 2015 is the day the riot police forcibly removed people in the first camps targeted – making them leave behind their possessions and destroying their homes and belongings to create 'an instant archeology of the migration crisis' (Davies and Isakjee 2015, 93) – this violence only punctuated a much longer process of domicide. The slow domicide resulting in 'The Jungle' included the displacement of food distribution, water points, and showers for migrants from the city itself to the abandoned children's camp Jules Ferry several kilometers outside. It also consisted of re-settling many of those who had already claimed asylum in Calais to other cities across France, the previously discussed rehousing of the women and families, and the daily harassment by police and workers of the French immigration office of those staying in the other autonomous camps and squats throughout the city (Calais Migrant Solidarity 2015b). These events did not occur without resistance, and many people chose to stay put despite the constant early morning threats by police to move further out of town or face arrest.

While the autonomous jungles were evicted and their inhabitants told to move down the road (the Centre Jules Ferry was located on the far side of what was an overground shrub-land at the end of Rue des Garennes along which hundreds of people were already staying), the occupations in the city center continued. Many people refused to leave their homes and live in the state's newly created 'tolerated zone'; citing distance from the city, environmental conditions, and the fear of police control (Calais Migrant

Solidarity 2015f). On June 2nd both the jungle out by the Eurotunnel terminal and a large squatted metal recycling facility – home to around four-hundred people and occupied for almost one year (Calais Migrant Solidarity 2017, 63) – were evicted by large numbers of police (Calais Migrant Solidarity 2015c). On September 22nd, the final evictions and destructions took place of the predominately Syrian groups remaining in the city and occupying a few locations. Those evicted in these actions were told by police to go to the jungle. They refused, sat down in the middle of the road and began chanting 'No Jungle! No Jungle!' (Calais Migrant Solidarity 2015d). The line of riot police reacted by tear-gassing the group and then frog-marching them for almost four kilometers all the way to the jungle (Solla and Menendez 2015). As they approached, those people camping along Rue des Garennes West of the A16 motorway bridge were also removed from their homes and had their tents destroyed by the same police line and pushed into the dune-land past the highway access ramp. This marked the elimination of all visible autonomous migrant occupations in the city and their consolidation into one territory where they were left to self-organize their living together in an increasingly shrinking space (Davies, Isakjee, and Dhesi 2017).

Seeing how the establishment of a migrant day center in Jules Ferry as well as the French state's tolerance of an autonomous migrant camp in its immediate surroundings also constituted domicide is crucial to understanding the current 'humanitarian' policing of migration extending across Europe. While this day center and 'tolerated jungle' was a new and seemingly positive development in the government response to the housing needs of illegalized border crossers in Calais, it was in fact tactic of segregation (Calais Migrant Solidarity 2015e; Tyerman 2016, 159–161) and part of a larger strategy to eliminate autonomous living spaces which might nurture anti-citizen politics (Calais Migrant Solidarity 2017, 64). As the number of arrivals increased during the 2015 'long summer of migration, so did the visible presence of migrants within Calais. Fearing the amount of people in Calais would continue to rise, Natacha Bouchart stated '[w]e think that the problem is going to get worse anyway so we need to do something to contain it. Perhaps the solution is to set up this centre … ' in her address to the House of Commons asking for UK funding for the project (Home Affairs Committee 2015, 6).

The Jules Ferry center was then explicitly conceived of as a tool of *containment* and migration governance and not service provision. It was a spatial technology of 'non-citizen' segregation as, faced with an unprecedented number of people and having fears of those numbers continuing to grow, the French government chose to provide specific (albeit extremely minimal) services to migrants in Calais in the hopes of concentrating them outside the city center. Accompanied by the overwhelming force of the police and their more naked acts of domicide, this new humanitarianism functioned to consolidate migrant occupations into one area, far from the city, and with access to the rest of city only provided by two roads which could easily be closed by police. In addition to serving as a means of mobility control through distancing migrants from points of crossing at the Eurotunnel – although there continued to be frequent attacks on the motorway leading to the port which passed right next to the jungle (Calais Migrant Solidarity 2018) – both the humanitarian face of the Jules Ferry center and the violent domicide of other occupations throughout the city 'worked to contain the migrant population outside the ordinary places and public spaces of *Calaisien* citizenship' (Tyerman 2016, 161). This carrot-and-stick domicide, having since been repeated with the CAOs, produced this jungle as a space of citizenship's enclosure and migration governance. While it is not within the scope of this article to present a detailed account of the evolution of this jungle nor the repression, domicide, autonomous actions, resistances, or anti-citizen solidarities of its residents, it is important to recognize 'The Jungle's' emergence as part of a state strategy to visibly segregate migrants at a time when the state's previous strategy of evictions without solutions became untenable.

5. Conclusion: seeing through erasure

It was an explicit decision in this article to focus upon citizenship as state exclusionary technology of migration governance and mobility control rather than elaborate on the spatial ruptures of migrants and their supporters. While it could be argued that focusing on state exclusionary practices reifies them, presents them as immutable, and denies the agency of those resisting them, this is not the intention behind the argument presented here. Rather than hardening the perception of France's border governance, carefully detailing domicide in Calais shows how the territorial segregation and destruction of communities of resistance is only the result of continuously reenacted state violence. It is only because of the constant disobedience and autonomy of illegalized border crossers that such a paranoid and hyperactive segregation exists today, with even the smallest spatial ruptures being stomped out quickly and over-whelmingly. From this current picture we can imagine the negative background of daily struggle by migrants to occupy and inhabit space in this city. Not elaborating upon the innumerable contentious forms of migrant inhabitance in Calais was done so as to allow the migrants themselves to decide how to tactically deploy the (in)visibility of their movements and spatial ruptures, and to contribute to redressing the amount of literature which expounds the politics of illegalized border crossers unsettling Europe's borders compared to that focusing on state repression. Each of the moments of domicide mentioned above was a reaction, and each of them are opportunities for researching and uncovering the resistant logics and spaces which have been erased.

By paying careful attention to state domicide, and its attempts to hide and obscure struggle, we can look beneath the givenness of the city-space of Calais in order to see how it has been cultivated to produce or prevent interactions between groups of people (e.g. residents and migrants, citizens and others). These interactions are governed by a regime of citizenship which orders space just as it is ordered by space. However, space is not atemporal but rather is fundamentally constructed by and through time, and is also fundamental in the construction of narrative and history. Recognizing temporality allows us to see beyond the flat surface of Calais as something already given, and allows for us to see how it has been created through struggle. María Lugones writes that 'to understand the spatiality of our lives is to understand that oppressing/being oppressed ⇔ resisting construct space simultaneously and that the temporality of each, at their infinite intersections, produces multiple histories/stories' (Lugones 2003, 12). By under-standing space as temporal it must be recognized that the erasure of the spatiality of resistance, in this case the domicide of anti-citizen inhabitance in Calais, is also an attempt to erase those histories of resistance.

These attempts at spatial and historical erasure of citizenship's 'others', and their stories of anti-citizen resistance, is an always incomplete task requiring constant reenactment.

Although today in Calais, due to the huge amount of resources the state has directed to constantly enacting domicidal interventions, it is difficult to imagine or reenact resistant spatial occupations (although they are nevertheless occurring). By paying close attention to how space and normative citizenship is constructed through the repression of dissident spatial ruptures, we can begin tracing the moves which have obscured resistances normative forms of citizenship and spatial inhabitance. By recognizing the interventions of domicide and the anti-coalitional citizenship logics which have produced the present, it is possible to begin scratching beneath the surface and discover the obscured and invisibilized resistant histories from which to take inspiration in the future.

Note

1. The city's squats and jungles can in one and the same time be places of segregation and exclusion, but also politicized spaces of struggle and resistance. They operate as a *technology of citizenship* as they 'deny and interrupt "presence" to people by hindering the visibility, association, recognition, status, and rights that come with being of the city' (Rygiel 2011, 14), while they also render hyper-visible people deemed to inhabit the camps when they are out in the city; produced as 'out of place' they are easily spotted, rounded up, detained, and sent back. However, these occupations are also collaboratively built and autonomously organized nodes in Papadopoulos and Tsianos' 'mobile commons' (King 2016, 107). This dual quality produces certain paradoxes in political organizing around such spaces. For example, 'The Jungle' existing between 2015–2016 was vehemently fought against when it was first proposed by the state as a 'tolerated' (and segregated) form of inhabitance, but then struggled *for* when faced with eviction (Ansems de Vries et al. 2017, 14–15).

Acknowledgments

My sincere thanks goes to the CAPPE Social Movements Network at the University of Brighton, friends and colleagues, and the two anonymous reviewers whose challenging and insightful feedback on earlier versions of this work were indispensable in helping to think through and revise this article.

Disclosure statement

No potential conflict of interest was reported by the author.

References

Anderson, B., N. Sharma, and C. Wright. 2009. "Editorial: Why No Borders?." *Refuge* 26 (2): 14.
Anderson, B., N. Sharma, and C. Wright. 2012. ""We are All Foreigners": No Borders as a Practical Political Project." In *Citizenship, Migrant Activism and the Politics of Movement*, edited by P. Nyers and K. Rygiel, 73–91. London: Routledge.

Ansems de Vries, L., and M. Welander. 2016. "Refugees, Displacement, and the European 'Politics of Exhaustion'." Sep. Accessed 05 May 2019. https://www.opendemocracy.net/en/mediterranean-journeys-in-hope/refugees-displacement-and-europ/

Ataç, I. 2016. "'Refugee Protest Camp Vienna': Making Citizens through Locations of the Protest Movement." *Citizenship Studies* 20 (5): 629–646. doi:10.1080/13621025.2016.1182676.

Ataç, I., K. Rygiel, and M. Stierl. 2016. "Introduction: The Contentious Politics of Refugee and Migrant Protest and Solidarity Movements: Remaking Citizenship from the Margins." *Citizenship Studies* 20 (5): 527–544. doi:10.1080/13621025.2016.1182681.

Balibar, E. 2009. "Europe as Borderland." *Environment and Planning D: Society and Space* 27 (2): 190–215. doi:10.1068/d13008.

Brandzel, A. L. 2016. *Against Citizenship: The Violence of the Normative*. Champaign, IL: University of Illinois Press.

Buchanan, S., and B. Grillo. 2004. "What's the Story?: Reporting on Asylum in the British Media." Forced Migration Review 19. http://www.fmreview.org/reproductive-health/buchanan-grillo.html

Bus, R. I. 2018a . "6 Forced Evictions Have Taken Place This Week in Calais. More than One a Day for the Period When These 'Operations' Can Be Conducted. Tents and Belongings Taken, No Solutions Provided #Calais #Humanrightspic.Twitter.Com/7jfb1fkcnr." Jun. Accessed 11 June 2018. https://twitter.com/RefugeeInfoBus/status/1002914036160266240

Calais Migrant Solidarity. 2013a. "Decision of Victor Hugo Given … but Not to Us!" Accessed 11 June 2018. https://calaismigrantsolidarity.wordpress.com/2013/11/20/decision-of-victor-hugo-given-but-not-to-us/

Calais Migrant Solidarity. 2013b. "No Eviction!" Dec. Accessed 11 June 2018. https://calaismigrantsolidarity.wordpress.com/2013/12/07/no-evacuation/

Calais Migrant Solidarity. 2015a. "Eviction Is a Process." Mar. Accessed 06 May 2018. https://calaismigrantsolidarity.wordpress.com/2015/03/29/eviction-is-a-process/

Calais Migrant Solidarity. 2015b. "The Evictions Have Started/Les Expulsions Ont Commencé." Mar. Accessed 09 June 2018. https://calaismigrantsolidarity.wordpress.com/2015/03/30/the-evictions-have-started/

Calais Migrant Solidarity. 2015c. "Evictions in Calais and Paris." Jun. Accessed 10 June 2018. https://calaismigrantsolidarity.wordpress.com/2015/06/02/evictions-in-calais-and-paris/

Calais Migrant Solidarity. 2015d. "Evictions: Last 5 Homes of Refugees in Calais Ville Destroyed, Apartheid Alive and Well in Calais." Sep. Accessed 17 December 2017. https://calaismigrantsolidarity.wordpress.com/2015/09/21/syrian-camp-destroyed-fascism-alive-and-well-in-calais/

Calais Migrant Solidarity. 2015e. "Jules Ferry Centre: Another Step Towards Segregation // Le Centre Jules Ferry: Un Autre Pas Vers La Segregation." Jan. Accessed 06 May 2018. https://calaismigrantsolidarity.wordpress.com/2015/01/29/jules-ferry-centre-another-steps-towards-segregation-le-centre-jules-ferry-un-autre-pas-vers-la-segregation/

Calais Migrant Solidarity. 2015f. "Why We are Not Moving; from Residents of Galloo." Apr. Accessed 10 June 2018. https://calaismigrantsolidarity.wordpress.com/2015/04/01/why-we-are-not-moving-from-residents-of-galloo/

Calais Migrant Solidarity. 2016. "Updates on Eviction in Calais." Oct. Accessed 03 October 2018. https://calaismigrantsolidarity.wordpress.com/2016/10/24/updates-on-eviction-in-calais/

Calais Migrant Solidarity. 2017. "Trapped on the Border: A Brief History of Solidarity Squatting Practices in Calais." In *Migration, Squatting and Radical Autonomy*, edited by P. Mudu and S. Chattopadhyay, 54–64. London and New York: Routledge.

Calais Migrant Solidarity. 2018. "'Riots' in the Jungle: Collective Refusal and Resistance in Calais." In *Riots and Militant Occupations: Smashing A System, Building A World - A Critical Introduction*, edited by A. Robinson and A. Starodub, 103–130. London: Rowman & Littlefield.

Calais Research. 2017. "Intro to Calais." Accessed 25 August 2018. https://calaisresearch.noblogs.org/intro-to-calais/

Calais Writers. 2017. *Voices from the 'Jungle': Stories from the Calais Refugee Camp*. London: Pluto Press.

Darling, J. 2017. "Acts, Ambiguities, and the Labour of Contesting Citizenship." *Citizenship Studies* 21 (6): 727–736. doi:10.1080/13621025.2017.1341658.

Davies, T., and A. Isakjee. 2015. "Geography, Migration and Abandonment in the Calais Refugee Camp." *Political Geography* 49: 93–95. doi:10.1016/j.polgeo.2015.08.003.

Davies, T., A. Isakjee, and S. Dhesi. 2017. "Violent Inaction: The Necropolitical Experience of Refugees in Europe." *Antipode* 49 (5): 1263–1284. doi:10.1111/anti.12325.

De Genova, N. 2007. "The Production of Culprits: From Deportability to Detainability in the Aftermath of "Homeland Security"." *Citizenship Studies* 11 (5): 421–448. doi:10.1080/13621020701605735.

De Genova, N. 2017. "Citizenship Shadow; Obscene Inclusion, Abject Belonging, Or, the Regularities of Migrant Irregularity." In *Within and beyond Citizenship: Borders, Membership and Belonging*, edited by R. G. Gonzales and N. Sigona, 17–35. Abingdon: Routledge.

de Vries, A., L. Leonie, M. Coleman, D. Rosenow, M. Tazzioli, and V. Rolando. 2017. "Fracturing Politics (Or, How to Avoid the Tacit Reproduction of Modern/Colonial Ontologies in Critical Thought)." *International Political Sociology* 11 (1): 90–108.

Délinquants Solidaires. 2018. "Délit De Solidarité: Une Association Accusée D'avoir Distribué Des Tentes À Calais." Mar. Accessed 19 May 2018. https://www.delinquantssolidaires.org/item/delit-de-solidarite-une-association-accusee-davoir-distribue-des-tentes-a-calais

Diaz, C., R. Ouali, O. Paquette, H. Masurel, M. Jamel, and M. Duclap. 2017. Evaluation de l'action Des Forces de l'ordre à Calais et Dans Le Dunkerquois. Technical Report. Inspection générale de la police nationale, Inspection générale de l'administration, Inspection générale de la gendarmerie nationale. https://www.interieur.gouv.fr/content/download/105744/837794/file/20171023%20-%20Rapport%20IGA-IGPN-IGGN(1).PDF

Douglas, P. J., and S. E. Smith. 2001. *Domicide: The Global Destruction of Home*. Montreal and Kingston: McGill-Queens University Press.

Figaro, L. 2015. "Renforcement De La Loi Contre Les Squatteurs." Le Figaro Accessed 29 April 2018 . http://www.lefigaro.fr/flash-actu/2015/06/11/97001-20150611FILWWW00298-renforcement-de-la-loi-contre-les-squatteurs.php

Fortier, A.-M. 2016. "Afterword: Acts of Affective Citizenship? Possibilities and Limitations." *Citizenship Studies* 20 (8): 1038–1044. doi:10.1080/13621025.2016.1229190.

Hindess, B. 2004. "Citizenship for All." *Citizenship Studies* 8 (3): 305–315. doi:10.1080/1362102042000257023.

Home Affairs Committee. 2015. "The Work of the Immigration Directorates: Calais Eighteenth Report of Session 2014-15." Technical Report. https://publications.parliament.uk/pa/cm201415/cmselect/cmhaff/902/902.pdf

Isin, E. F. 2002. *Being Political: Genealogies of Citizenship*. Minneapolis, MN: University of Minnesota Press.

Isin, E. F., and G. M. Nielsen. 2008. *Acts of Citizenship*. London: Zed Books.

King, N. 2016. *No Borders: The Politics of Immigration Controls and Resistance*. London: Zed Books.

L'Auberge des Migrants, Utopia 56, Help Refugees, and Refugee Info Bus. 2018. "Police Violence in Calais: Abusive and Illegal Practices by Law Enforcement Officers." Technical Report. Accessed 12 January 2018. https://helprefugees.org/wp-content/uploads/2018/08/Police-Harrassment-of-Volunteers-in-Calais-1.pdf

La Voix du Nord. 2014a. "Calais : Le Squat Victor-Hugo Sera Libéré La Semaine Prochaine." Jun. Accessed 11 June 2018. http://www.lavoixdunord.fr/archive/recup%3A%252Fregion%252Fcalais-le-squat-victor-hugo-sera-libere-la-semaine-prochaine-ia33b0n2239894

La Voix du Nord. 2014b. "Squat Victor-Hugo À Calais : L'association Solid'R a Commencé À Rencontrer Les Femmes Migrantes." May. Accessed 11 June 2018. http://www.lavoixdunord.fr/archive/recup/region/squat-victor-hugo-a-calais-l-association-solid-r-a-ia33b48581n2156212

Lugones, M. 2003. *Pilgrimages/Peregrinajes: Theorizing Coalition Against Multiple Oppressions*. Lanham, MD: Rowman & Littlefield.

Maestri, G., and S. M. Hughes. 2017. "Contested Spaces of Citizenship: Camps, Borders, and Urban Encounters." *Citizenship Studies* 21 (6): 625–639. doi:10.1080/13621025.2017.1341657.

Mezzadra, S., and B. Neilson. 2013. *Border as Method, Or, the Multiplication of Labor*. Durham and London: Duke University Press.

Mould, O. 2017a. "The Calais Jungle: A Slum of London's Making." *City* 21 (3–4): 388–404. doi:10.1080/13604813.2017.1325231.

Mould, O. 2017b. "The Not-so-Concrete Jungle: Material Precarity in the Calais Refugee Camp." *Cultural Geographies* 25 (3): 1–7.

Mudu, P., and S. Chattopadhyay, eds. 2017. *Migration, Squatting and Radical Autonomy*. London and New York: Routledge.

Nowicki, M. 2014. "Rethinking Domicide: Towards an Expanded Critical Geography of Home: Rethinking Domicide." *Geography Compass* 8 (11): 785–795. doi:10.1111/gec3.v8.11.

Nowicki, M. 2017. "Domicide and the Coalition: Austerity, Citizenship and Moralities of Forced Eviction in Inner London." In *Geographies of Forced Eviction: Dispossession, Violence, Resistance*, edited by K. Brickell, M. F. Arrigoitia, and A. Vasudevan, 121–143. London: Palgrave Macmillan.

Nyers, P. 2015. "Migrant Citizenships and Autonomous Mobilities." *Migration, Mobility, & Displacement* 1 (1). doi:10.18357/mmd11201513521.

Nyers, P., and K. Rygiel, eds. 2012. *Citizenship, Migrant Activism and the Politics of Movement*. Abingdon: Routledge.

Papadopoulos, D., and V. Tsianos. 2013. "After Citizenship: Autonomy of Migration, Organisational Ontology and Mobile Commons." *Citizenship Studies* 17 (2): 178–196. doi:10.1080/13621025.2013.780736.

Refugee Info Bus. 2018b. "Over the Weekend, French Police Came to 2 Living Places in Calais with Sharp Objects and Destroyed Tents, Whilst People Went to Access Breakfast Distributions. These Destructions are Inhumane and Illegal #Calais #Humanrightsviolationspic.Twitter.Com/Ondmldxv6t." May. Accessed 11 June 2018. https://twitter.com/RefugeeInfoBus/status/1001354123579621376

Refugee Info Bus. 2018c . "Yesterday, Another Forced Eviction Took Place at a Living Point, in Calais. These Evictions Take Place between 3-5 Times a Week. Here, a 15 Year Old Minor Explains to Police that His Food Is inside the Tent that Is Being Illegally Taken Away #Humanrights #Calais #Refugeespic.Twitter.Com/Wef4stcebj." May. Accessed 11 June 2018. https://twitter.com/RefugeeInfoBus/status/999667564170108928

Reuters. 2016. "Empty Makeshift Shelters Burn in Calais "Jungle"." Oct. Accessed 03 October 2018 2018. https://reuters.screenocean.com/record/83755

Rigby, J., and R. Schlembach. 2013. "Impossible Protest: Noborders in Calais." *Citizenship Studies* 17 (2): 157–172. doi:10.1080/13621025.2013.780731.

Rygiel, K. 2011. "Bordering Solidarities: Migrant Activism and the Politics of Movement and Camps at Calais." *Citizenship Studies* 15 (1): 1–19. doi:10.1080/13621025.2011.534911.

Solla, A., and C. Menendez. 2015. "French Police Use Teargas on Refugees in Calais – Video." *The Guardian* Accessed 10 June 2018. http://www.theguardian.com/world/video/2015/sep/22/french-police-use-teargas-on-refugees-in-calais-video

Tazzioli, M. 2017a. "Beyond Citizen Politics." In *Tunisia as a Revolutionized Space of Migration*, Mobility & Politics G. Garelli and M. Tazzioli edited by, 69–88. New York, NY: Palgrave Pivot.

Tazzioli, M. 2017b. "Calais after the Jungle: Migrant Dispersal and the Expulsion of Humanitarianism." Jul. Accessed 20 August 2018. https://www.opendemocracy.net/beyondslavery/martina-tazzioli/calais-after-jungle-migrant-dispersal-and-expulsion-of-humanitarianis

Tyerman, T. 2016. "Border Struggles : Segregation, Migrant Solidarity, and Ethical Politics in Everyday Life." PhD Thesis, University of Manchester. http://ethos.bl.uk/OrderDetails.do?uin=uk.bl.ethos.722300

Vincent, E. 2014. "Calais Va Rouvrir Un Centre D'accueil Pour Migrants." Le Monde.fr Accessed 10 June 2018. https://www.lemonde.fr/societe/article/2014/09/03/calais-va-rouvrir-un-centre-d-accueil-pour-migrants_4480871_3224.html

Willsher, K. 2018. "France Will Not Allow Another Refugee Camp in Calais, Says Macron; French President Warns People Trying to Reach UK from Northern France that They are at 'Dead End'." *The Guardian*.

Migrants' inhabiting through commoning and state enclosures. A postface

Massimo De Angelis

ABSTRACT

In this paper, I deploy the framework of commons as social systems which I have developed in my last book *Omnia Sunt Communia* to interpret the debate developed in this issue, enquire on the relationship between commons and citizenship, and ground the question of migrants' inhabiting on the theory of commoning.

Migrants' commons

Starting from the proposition that we should not confuse the commons with resources held in common, I approach commons as social systems in which resources are pooled by a community of subjects who *also* govern communally these resources and the social reproduction of the community, and who engage in commoning, a form of social labour that has a direct relation to the needs, desires and aspirations of the commoners in given contexts. Through commoning, subjects create these conditions of existence and self-orientation through self-organisation and may develop from grassroots into more all-encompassing systems. Thus, commons come in many shapes and sizes.

In this collection, we see the commons creeping in migrant housing squats in Rome (Montagna and Grazioli 2019) and in Athens (Raimondi 2019), in temporary self-made shelters built next to a refugee camp so as to strategically capture electricity, or even as self-organisation inside the camp in West Balkans (Stojic Mitrovic and Vilenica 2019), and in the refugees *inhabiting* of the city *by* waiving relations with social movements (Dadusc et al. 2019; Dadusc 2019). It is also visible, as in a mirror image, in the strategies of enclosures of the self-created domicile, what Van Isacker (2019) calls 'domicide'. In this essay, I wish to read some of the arguments presented in this collection through the lens of the commons as systems (De Angelis 2017), their boundaries and their diverse relations with other actors within their environments.

(1) The different types of commons all reproduce certain basic elements, at least in their general sense. Thus, at a general organisational level, in order to have commons – of whatever type – we need to have at least three constituent elements, the dry specification of life-enhancing, organic development, a socio-ecological, metabolic process in which cultures of sharing are (re)produced:

(2) Pooled resources (material and/or immaterial)

(3) A community of commoners, that is, subjects willing to share, pool and reproduce the resources that require reproduction (not necessarily a local community in the classical sense of village, territory, etc.)

(4) Commoning.

The life-blood of the commons, its dynamic energy and first source of its power and form, is the process of commoning, doing in common. In his book *The Magna Carta Manifesto*, historian Peter Linebaugh (2008) traces the origin and development of this crucial constitutional text as emerging from the commoners' struggle to have their rights to the commons recognised and acknowledged by the state. In this context, commoning is the activity of the commoners in organic relation to the 'commons' (as pooled resources that need to be sustained and reproduced) and to one another. This implies that commoning is an *activity* that develops *relations preoccupied by their (re) production* and therefore crucially founded on their own autonomy vis-a-vis their environment: the state is one of the ever-present entities in the environment of the commons, and so as other commons, other social movements and other systems. Commoning thus is an ongoing flow constituent of rights, common rights, which are not 'granted' by the state, by the powerful, but that originate in their *being exercised*, so as the state can only, at most, acknowledge and confirm them, or else deny and restrict them. Commoning thus occurs *within, against and beyond citizenship*, depending who are the subjects of commoning in different contexts, and depending on the observation points.

In this special issue we have seen how the rights of the migrant's commons have been denied in hypercycles of enclosure and control, but also, how more difficult it becomes for the state to deny and restrict these rights when migrants self-organize together with social movements and activists.

Different elements of this are illustrated in different measures by all papers in this collection. Perhaps more significant to outline the commons in this special issue are the interventions by Montagna and Grazioli on migrants in Rome, Raimondi in the migrant housing squats in Exarchia in Athens, as well as Dadusc in the Netherlands squatted buildings. In all these cases is the strict relationship between migrants and networks of activists (citizens) who provide support by sharing 'their toolbox of care, political and organisational practices' (Montagna and Grazioli 2019, 579). The cases of the Quattro Stelle Occupato and Baobab in Rome represent different modulations of commons, whose phenomenology, which is always grounded in the vast array of needs of social reproduction in different contexts, corresponds to different priorities: housing and daily reproduction in the first case, supported by 'non-discriminatory ground rules coming from the Housing Rights Movements' (ibid) to allow effective communal decision-making, and to support migrants' mobility in the second. In the case of The Netherlands squatted *homes* 'work as spaces to create different social, political and affective relations based on solidarity, cooperation and mutual aid' (Dadusc 2019, 598).

These cases may be identifying 'mobile commons' (Montagna and Grazioli 2019; Mezzadra and Neilson 2013) as the commons represent an infrastructure to enable migrants' mobility, which include the rest. I think it would be also appropriate to talk about liminal commons (Varvarousis 2018, or similarly in terms of the notion of temporary autonomous zones as in Bey 1991); that is, commons spaces that are temporary in nature for the migrants, and maybe temporary as particular places, and that enable them to reproduce their life and live through relations of care, solidarity and sociability and/or empowering them with the knowledge and tricks of survival while waiting for the opportunity to engage with the *game* (*see* Stojić Mitrović and Vilenica 2019) of attempting to move on, and to reach and cross the border. These types of commons also mark migrants' subjectivities with memory of solidarity values and affects.

In any case, the commons of Rome, Athens and the Netherlands discussed in this collection demonstrate that through the activity of commoning, which also engages networks of activists, migrants achieve higher protection and more livable lives within the context of their journey. To a large extent, the power emerging from commoning emerges from *boundary commoning*, that 'structural coupling' between systems (De Angelis 2017) emerging out of the continuous interaction among them, as in the case of the one established on a continuous basis among migrants and networks of activists. In the case discussed by Raimondi in Exarchia, this connection enables migrants to mobilize significant defence power against the incursions of fascists and the police. Boundary commoning allows greater reach, the sharing of a more diverse pool of material and immaterial resources, while leading to more complexity at disposal of the migrant commons. For example, in the case of Baobab, 'the network of activists, grassroots movements, NGOs and associations … provides healthcare services, legal assistance, advise on the safest routes to Europe, alphabetization and counselling about job opportunities' (Montagna and Grazioli 2019, 568). However, 'Baobab is not only a top-down kind of solidarity organized by the activists for the migrants in a state of need. Although the bare bone of activists and volunteers is made of Italians, as soon as migrants arrive and even if they are only transient and stay temporarily, they are asked to participate in the management of the camp according to their capabilities' (ibid.). This collaboration gives way to the construction of a more diverse organization, and therefore of superior complexity. Because of this superior complexity, they can collectively command more social power (De Angelis 2017, 357–388).

Thus, migrants enter *4 Stelle* and exit as reproduced in body and spirit, with a wealth of encounters and emotionally recharged. They enter Baobab and exit it with know-how. They enter the migrant squat in Exarchia, and they are much safer than outside it. The commons mark the migrant subjectivities in ways to empower them to better navigate the complexity of their journey. While the structures of the state aim at controlling the migrants as rights-less, these commons socially reproduce them as migrants through commons rights, and the boundary commoning therein (re)produce new subjectivities: 'silent individuals, who needed to hide and who lived in a conditions of constant fear, became active and powerful collectives, appropriating and inhabiting urban, social and political spaces, creating collective platforms to challenge the micropolitics of border regimes' (Dadusc 2019, 599) and 'hybrid political subjectivity between migrant and non-migrant' are produced 'with breaking existing barriers' (Raimondi 2019, 568).

A counter case is that of shelters in Rome discussed here by Grazioli and Montagna in which migrants did not self-organize but hide away trapped in between inner seclusion and outer policing and were not able to enact any resistance to eviction nor articulate demands. The power that emerges out of commoning and 'boundary commoning' creates a force field whose boundaries create a filter, allowing in those flows of solidarity and exchange constituting 'boundary commoning', while filtering out to a various degree the control and domicidal tactics of the state (Van Isacker 2019). Interestingly, a specular movement emerge on the other side of the 'citizenship' divide. In state borders and borderscapes (as in Stojić Mitrović and Vilenica 2019), there is also a filtering. While borders emerge out of a historical accumulation of conflict between nation states subjugating commoners to their causes, contemporary European borderscapes emerge out of an ongoing attempt to control the flows of migrants, while leaving open the flows of regular citizens. Borderscapes are thus, in the sense, the result of a daily struggle, migrants outsmarting the state and the perturbed state devising new control systems, which include both the criminalisation and securitisation apparatus of the state and its 'humanitarian' counterpart, modes of governance of migrants' bodies, lives and voices 'victimising them as vulnerable objects of lack and of need' (Dadusc 2019, 596). Also, the boundaries of the migrants-commons are the result of a daily struggle, just from the 'non-citizen' perspective, they are formed through the commoning that involve inhabiting these spaces and social relationships, and open up spaces against and beyond the 'micropolitics of the border' and borderscapes, with its 'coercive modes of power, disciplinary power and biopower' (Dadusc 2019, 596).

Autonomy, power and boundary commoning

The quality, filtering mechanism and strength of the commons boundary is the result of the autonomous activity of commoning, the properties of the networks it mobilises, and the values it practices (De Angelis 2017). In the cases discussed here, the commons boundary is the result of migrant-commoners that take things in their own hands in respect of certain material or cultural aspects of their (re)production, survival and plans. They are autonomous here vis-a-vis the state, they self-determine in their own interactions, orientations and social exchanges and, in this way, they strive to escape its diffused borderscape. Therefore, in their own dissent, these commons grounded on their context-specific social reproduction, are in the most virtuous sense, political.

This social autonomous force mobilized by commoning has both a quantitative and qualitative dimension, two sides of the same process. The former concerns the amount of commons resources and numbers of migrant and activist commoners mobilized within a given space, the measure of the force field (in term of both material and immaterial elements) enacted through commoning vis a vis the capacity of mobilization of the state. This quantitative dimension of autonomy is an emergent condition and a strategic problem of development. For the qualitative dimension of autonomy, I borrow from the evolutionary biologist Varela. For Varela autonomous systems are 'defined as a composite unity by a network of interactions of components that (i) through their interactions recursively regenerate the network of interactions that produced them, and (ii) realise the network as a unity in the space in which the components exist by constituting and specifying the unity's boundaries as a cleavage from the background' (Varela 1981, 15). Through commoning, the material and the immaterial components of commons networks – the migrants, the activists, the buildings, the food, the know-how, the affects, the imaginary, the memories, the stories, the hopes and the fears – do not lie dormant as subjugated victims or derelict spaces but 'their interaction recursively regenerate the network of interaction that generated them' and in doing so they 'realise the network interactions that produced them as a unity in the space in which the components exist by constituting and specifying the unity's boundaries as a cleavage from the background' (Varela 1981, 15).

A boundary is formed by the very autonomous self-activity of the commoners which establish recursively a force field and therefore a boundary. On this ground, the political question is always one with the expansion of the commons ecology of solidarity and reproduction. Politics here does not mediate anything, it is the direct positing of a social force for the production of life, and *hegemony* would coincide with a *state* of transformation, not a condition necessary for transformation. The struggle and commons of migrants make this point very clear. Unlike the products of conventional politics, the hierarchically controlled humanitarian and state-run shelters, migrants inhabiting a place through commoning and solidarity becomes a terrain of struggle. It is a condition similar to the one lived and experienced by Amazonian indigenous people, or the Palestinian condition, or any other subjectivities for long periods of time at the frontline of value struggle vis-à-vis capital and the state, where existence coincides with resistance and, with no or very little mediations, the *conditions* of existence are the results of past resistance. The notion presented in this collection of 'inhabitance' intended as 'a practice of urban commoning through creation of kinship networks and communities as a form of resistance to the violence, isolation and segregation of both securitarian and humanitarian enclosures' (Dadusc 2019, 594) precisely indicates this condition of existence as resistance.

It is also important to recognize that as these commoning practices are not confined within the boundaries of citizenship but they create their own boundaries, they escape citizenship, they go beyond it even if the power of these practices increases with the presence of citizens as part of the inhabitance network. To clarify this point, let us turn to the environment of the migrant commons. At a very general level, leaving aside ecological systems, there are four main systems in the environment of inhabiting migrant commons: the state; organized network of activists; organized networks of xenophobic anti-migrants; the 'public' (for lack of better words). The state is a system of systems, a holon but organized hierarchically. The term *holon* derives from 'the greek holos = whole, with the suffix on which, as in proton and neutron, suggest a particular part' (Koestler 1967, 48). Holons thus are systems within systems making nested sequences of parts and whole. Each entity we focus on, a migrant collective, a city, a neighbourhood, thus, has an upward series of holons of which it is part, and a downward series of nested and interacting holons, of which it is composed. In so far as migrants are concerned, upward holons are constituted of police, tribunals, and the repressive-administrative apparatus on one side, and the health service and NGOs and Charities (or 'civil society') on the other, both organized hierarchically although to a different degree. At any moment of their journey, the gaze from the migrant commons outwards, see citizenship as technology of control. It is a gaze that anticipate the policemen looking for your papers, the NGO checking you have not arrived late at a camp, the noise of the police arriving with bulldozers and pepper spray at their makeshift camp to implement domicide, a diffused technology that aims at controlling the non-citizen migrants' complexity, its distinctive variety, and harass it, threaten it, channel it, control it.

The network of activists, as we have seen, by virtue of being empowered by a citizenship status, consists in all those systems of mutual aid and solidarity that use this power to help migrants in their journey of social reproduction. Their relationship with migrants is not of *citizenship*, as they do not represent the state, nor, if they even formally do, intend to implement the logic of its control technology. Their relationship is more vernacular, and one of commoning, expressing value practices that escape the control and the boundaries of citizenship. These networks often clash with the network of anti-migrants, those fascist, racist and xenophobic forces who are enchanted by the 'nationals first', and disseminate lies and hate forgetting how capitalist globalization, wars, culture and climate change has eroded the boundaries for all matters concerning life and survival, including theirs. Finally, I call the 'public' here as the remaining areas of society, segmented by income and wealth and to a certain extent normalised to the systems of life reproduction they are engaged in and made busy by its multiple deadlines. They are made of the people who pass by, who witness and often are bystanders, who may give resonance to the reasons of migrants and their allied networks of activists, or to those of the state, or to those of the fascist and racists and *national first*.

To complicate this picture there is the fact that individuals or groups of commoners sympathizing with migrants could be also located in any of these systems or even more than one. A doctor working in the health service (state), a teacher working in a school, could also be part of a network of activists offering solidarity to a migrant commons, as silent members of the public may – in given context – come out with acts of solidarity and a policemen could 'forget' to ask for papers, and a youth find the violence of the racist language of his fascists mates no longer bearable, a mayor could make sure that migrants in a city are part of an alternative model of development based on their inclusion and support. Through the boundaries of all these systems in the environment of the migrant commons, there are ongoing flows of internal movement, deterritorialisation and re-territorialisation.

Let us go back to the state and its bordering practices or borderscapes. The state has two broad strategies vis a vis the commons, and these are enclosures and cooptation. With the first it aims at destroy them, disperse the material and immaterial elements within them and undermine the condition of social reproduction of the bodies within them, in this case, first of all, of migrants. With cooptation, the state aims at capturing selected elements of social reproduction present in the commons, but in ways that serve the purpose of governmentality of social flows and control strategies. In most of the interventions in this collection, these two moments are intertwined.

State enclosures

The term 'enclosure' is a short and evocative name to refer to the 'original accumulation' necessary as a precondition of accumulation (Marx 1976). Every process of accumulation – and therefore of governance of workers/citizens' subjectivities – requires that workers are available and willing to subject themselves to the disciplinary mechanism of capitalist work, and that means of production are concentrated in the hands of capitalists. In traditional Marxist literature, this original accumulation was seen as happening once and for all at the beginning of a historical process of accumulation, although Marx himself might have opened for a broader and more continuous understanding of original accumulation in capitalism (De

Angelis 2001). In the 1990s and early 2000s, pushed by the need to interpret the process of attack on welfare rights, wages, pensions, union rights and structural adjustment that emerged since the end of the 1970s, some authors (Midnight Notes Collective 1990; De Angelis 2001, 2004 and, from a different framework, Harvey 2003) began to interpret this as moment of original accumulation, which then was no longer confined at a distant moment in history before capitalism, but as an ongoing presence within capitalist relations, a strategy that state and capital could mobilize to reactivate a process of accumulation. This 'continuous character of enclosure' can, of course, be adapted to particular contexts and strategic objectives by the state/capital but is an ever-present threat we should be alerted.

In this special issue, enclosure has appeared in many ways, from the cases of domicide strategies of camp/squat destruction, to the ever-present threat of deportation, we are in presence of given examples of enclosures. For example, in Van Isacker's contribution in this collection, the notion of enclosure is captured by that of *domicide* 'as a technology of citizenship; a means through which normative citizenship becomes spatialized, forms of inhabitance furnishing anti-citizen solidarities and politics eliminated, and "non-citizens" directed into spaces requiring them to submit to the scrutiny of the citizenship regime and abandon their onward journeys' (Van Isacker 2019). In Dadusc's contribution (2019, 596) enclosures take on a variety of objectives: 'from spatial segregation (spatial enclosures), intervention on migrants' bodies and everyday lives (affective enclosures), taming migrants' struggles (humanitarian enclosure) as well as diverting the attention from the structural harms and violence of borders (epistemic enclosure)'. These enclosures, i.e. extra-economic expropriation of resources, or erection of barriers to social networks and affects, or to prevent the naked truth about state operations to emerge, are the preconditions for the government of 'undocumented migrants, as well as citizens' and are the manifestation of conditions of securitisation which together with the deployment of 'humanitarian borders' (or cooptation) allow migrants to be '*constantly* governed at distance through interventions in their everyday lives and affective relations, and are kept in a condition of fear, invisibility, silence and dependency' (ibid, 596) and reproduce their condition of precarity and subjection together with exclusion and rejection (Anderson, Sharma, and Wright 2009; Mezzadra and Neilson 2013).

As I pointed out (De Angelis 2007, 2017) enclosures (as well as cooptation) and the commons, do not simply rest as static binaries. They are instead locked in a continuous cycle, ongoing battle, in which the state/capital element of the binary enforces enclosures to decompose the social composition of social movements which then, in time recreate its strength to a new pattern of recomposition to attack state/capital in a different context and historical moment. In some of the cases in this collection, for example, in Van Isacker's and Stojić Mitrović and Vilenica's contributions, we are in presence of hypercycles, in which the state accelerate this temporal dimension of this process of decomposition, and migrants adapt with ongoing attempt of recomposition with their return to jungles or camps, while the number of migrants accumulate either for continuous inflows and/or for the returnees return to the camp or squats for unsuccessful border crossing. These processes are context specific and define different objectives by the state. While in the case of Calais this process of continuously erasing 'autonomous modes of inhabitance', find its rationale in the French state objective that migrants 'enter into the spatial circuits of citizenship, and submit to the scrutiny of the asylum and regularization process' (Van Isacker 2019, 617), in the case of the Western

Balkan states, the cycle is accelerated also as 'a consequence of economic dependence of Serbian migration management on the funds from the EU' (Stojić Mitrović and Vilenica 2019, 551). Thus, the self-organised camp attached to the official camp becomes an important buffer from which to regularly raid for migrants' bodies to be brought into the official camp, in order to maintain this to full capacity and therefore been able to claim the full amount of compensation from the EU.

The enclosures and the re-appropriation therefore follow a hypercycle, the continuous character of enclosures is accelerating, as much as commons reformation which can never reach critical point because of rapid incoming enclosures. It is in the conditions of this hyper-cycle that constitutes 'the negative background of daily struggle by migrants to occupy and inhabit space in this city' (Van Isacker 2019, 621) which enforces conditions of precarity as the basic core of accelerated state enclosures, as a state reaction to the logic and patterns of resistance of migrants. Nobody knows how long will this precarity-inducing hypercycle of enclosures last. What we know is that limiting freedom, does not promote 'inclusion'. The state also seeks control of the micro commons established inside official (or NGO) hosting infrastructure, with strict rules limiting movement, or sudden appearance of NGO officers or police to inhabited space to control whether rules are followed (including the prohibition to host people in their room or shared apartments). In this way, the flow of solidarity is cut, the migrants are the target of domesticated strategies, their freedom reduced. However, when in some location and context the state is able to impose its hypercycles of enclosures as a locus of concentrated social forces, in many others, migrants are taking the upper ends, and are able to organize in autonomous housing squats and opt out the official system.

Citizenship and the commons

In this collection, different notions of citizenship have been explored, as a reflection of current literature or a contribution to it. Reading this debate from the perspective of the commons, what is evident is that the various forms of citizenship employed are particular forms of relationships, in which commoners are transfigured into citizens by the very fact they relate to the state. In this sense, at any given time, citizenship is an accumulation of rights and duties vis-à-vis the state which have come about as stratification of the outcome of past struggles, attritions and maneuvers. In other words, acts of citizenship enacted in the past. Acts of citizenship therefore only exist ex-post, only when they have been recognized and co-opted into new exclusions, and they are intertwined in the new habitus of citizenship. Ex-ante we are only in the realm of 'prefigured' citizenship, which actualization, i.e. recognition with a deal within the state, may or may never come, or if it does happen, it happens together with forms of exclusion that are not anticipated by the 'actors' of citizenship.

If acts of citizenship break the habitus of citizenship to push to evolve citizenship into a new habitus, a relationship of anti-citizenship refuses this all together (Van Isacker 2019). As we have seen, in this collection anti-citizenship emerges as a concept to define a refusal of the bipolar enclosure/cooptation strategies adopted by the French state, to take one example, to control flows of migrants into the official camp, which confines migrants to either apply for refugees status in France or be deported, while receiving all range of humanitarian support. A refusal also to desist to make camp while waiting for the right opportunity to 'join the game' and cross the border into the UK. The French state repeated the violent strategy of domicide (enclosure) as a mirror image of the migrant attitude of anti-citizenship. However, the clashing polarity domicide (state tactics) anti-citizenship (migrant-perspective) is a polarity that exists only in the landscape on the prohibited border or diffused borderscape and at this *level* of *social systemic interaction*. Within the repeated hypercycles of domicides and inhabitance formation (enclosures-commons), there is a ripple of individual subjects which escape and are able to cross the border to the UK. Another ripple from these that claim asylum and are successfully awarded 'leave to remain' and, after five years, apply for citizenship and maybe obtaining it. For these subset of individual migrants, their anti-citizenship practices at the French border count as a moment in a long journey which ends, if they are lucky and so desire, towards citizenship. The carrot is always there. Whatever is the technology of control the migrants have faced in their journey, at any moment of this they also engage in some form of commoning to reproduce their life and that of others they have encountered.

Citizenship is a state of inclusion within a given order, given rights and obligations. Commoning is an activity whose praxis is always defined by the commoners themselves, an activity that produces autonomy in different contexts and in different degrees. The notions of commons and commoning do not necessarily require that of citizenship, while on the contrary, that of citizenship, at any given time, is a deal between the state and various social forces, in which the commons in movement have played a crucial role. At any given moment, commons and commoning are a condition of existence of citizenship. Think about what the state would be without the commoning involved in social reproduction. On the other hand, citizenship is a set of enabling rights and constraining duties put on individuals, as citizens, and on their forms of commoning. Commons are self-governing, but citizenship represents an externally enforced limit which may or may not be overcome by particular types of commoning, and this depends on the social force(s) it mobilizes. Commoning could as well become acts of citizenship and be able to change these constraints, but it is not limited to this. Indeed, it has been shown that commoning could also happen among non-citizens, or non-citizens and citizens (as among migrants and networks of activists) and thus escape from the constrains of citizenship while striving to reproducing life. Whether this boundary commoning will serve to change the notion of citizenship in the future that is, retrospectively to be recognized as act of citizenship, is irrelevant to the immanence of commoning. In the here and now, in the daily challenge of migrants' social reproduction, commoning emerges as a way to facilitate existence while increasing the power of resistance.

Disclosure statement

No potential conflict of interest was reported by the author.

References

Anderson, B., N. Sharma, and C. Wright. 2009. "Editorial: Why No Borders?" *Refuge: Canada's Journal on Refugees* 26: 5–18.

Bey, H. 1991. *Temporary Autonomous Zones*. New York: Autonomedia.

Dadusc, D. 2019. "The micropolitics of border struggles." *Citizenship Studies* 23 (6).

Dadusc, D., M. Grazioli, and M. A. Martínez. 2019. "Citizenship as inhabitance? Migrant housing squats versus the proliferation of camps." *Citizenship Studies* 23 (6).

De Angelis, M. 2001. "Marx and primitive accumulation: The continuous character of capital's "enclosures"." *In The Commoner* N. 2, September http://www.commoner.org.uk/02deangelis.pdf

De Angelis, M. 2004. "Separating the Doing and the Deed: Capital and the Continuous Character of Enclosures." *Historical Materialism* 12 (2): 57–87. doi:10.1163/1569206041551609.

De Angelis, M. 2007. *The Beginning of History. Global Capital and Value Struggles*. London: Pluto.

De Angelis, M. 2017. *Omnia Sunt Communia. On the Commons and the Transformation to Postcapitalism*. London: Zed books.

Grazioli, M., and N. Montagna. 2019. "Urban commons and freedom of movement: The housing struggles of recently arrived migrants and refugees in Rome." *Citizenship Studies* 23 (6).

Harvey, D. 2003. *The New Imperialism*. Oxford: Oxford University Press.

Koestler, A. 1967. *The Ghost in the Machine*. London: Hutchinson.

Linebaugh, P. 2008. *The Magna Carta Manifesto: Liberties and commons for all*. Berkeley: University of California Press.

Marx, K. 1976. *Capital. A Critique of Political Economy*. Vol. 1. New York: Penguin Books.

Mezzadra, S., and B. Neilson. 2013. *Border as Method, or, the Multiplication of Labor*. Durham and London: Duke University Press.

Midnight Notes Collective. 1990. *New Enclosures*. Midnight Notes, (10). http://www.midnightnotes.org/newenclos.html

Raimondi, V. 2019. "'For common struggles of migrants and locals'. Experiences of squatting between local and migrant activists in Athens." *Citizenship Studies* 23 (6).

Stojić Mitrović, M., and A. Vilenica. 2019. "Enforcing and Disrupting Circular Movement in an EU Borderscape: Housingscaping in Serbia." *Citizenship Studies* 23 (6).

Van Isacker, T. 2019. "Bordering through domicide: Spatializing citizenship in Calais." *Citizenship Studies* 23 (6).

Varela, F. J. 1981. "Autonomy and Autopoiesis." In *Self- Organizing Systems: An Interdisciplinary Approach*, edited by G. Roth and H. Schwegler, 14–24. Frankfurt and New York: Campus verlag.

Varvarousis, A. 2018. *Crisis, Commons & Liminality. Modern Rituals of Transition in Greece*. PhD Thesis. Universitat Autonoma de Barcelona.

Index

Note: Page numbers followed by 'n' refers to end notes.